On Flows the Tay

'*I believe that the main features of the war can be more accurately seen and more truly judged by those who live through it than by a scholar writing after the lapse of half a century.*'

John Buchan

Dr Bill Harding, Ph.D., F.E.I.S.

Although born in Angus, Bill Harding was brought up in Perth. Educated at Perth Academy and Aberdeen University, he worked as teacher, lecturer and researcher, both at home and abroad, during which time he graduated from the Universities of London, St Andrews, Dundee, Glasgow and Strathclyde. A Fellow of the Educational Institute of Scotland, he won a Page Scholarship to the United States. Unfortunately, ill health forced his early retirement. This, however, did not put an end to his research and writing. *On Flows the Tay* resulted from his interest in the relationship between war and social change.

On Flows the Tay

Perth and the First World War

Dr Bill Harding

Cualann Press

ISBN 0 9535036 2 3

First Edition 2000

British Library in Publication Data. A catalogue record of this book is available at the British Library

Printed by Bell & Bain, Glasgow

On Flows the Tay is the third book in the *Voices of War* series published by

**Cualann Press, 6 Corpach Drive, Dunfermline, Fife, KY12 7XG, Scotland
Email cualann@ouvip.com Website http://users.ouvip.com/cualann/**

ACKNOWLEDGEMENTS

This work would not have been possible without the aid of Steve Connelly, Archivist, Perth Archive Unit, A K Bell Library, Perth. He led me through a labyrinth of files and records, many of which had not seen the light of day for over eighty years. His colleagues, Jeremy Duncan in the Local History Library and Bob Mairs and John Campbell in the Lending Library, were equally helpful in tracking down obscure references and articles. A special thanks is due to my 'old friends' in Perth who helped me capture the mood of the First World War.

Of considerable interest were the contributions of three elderly Perth residents: Mrs Isa Reeve, Miss Janet Dalgleish and Mr Dick Muirhead. Mrs Isa Reeve (née Gow), born in 1899, recalled the excitement of 1914 but remembered the war years in general as 'a sad time', her family short of food and the streets full of amputees in 1919. She remembered thinking that all Germans, especially organ-grinders, were spies and that Perth would be invaded almost any day. Mr Dick Muirhead, born in 1901, enlisted 'for a lark' with four friends on a Saturday afternoon jaunt to Dundee. He joined the Royal Navy as a teenage gun-loader on HMS *Canada* at Harwich. His four friends who joined the Black Watch were killed in action. Dick survived the Battle of Jutland in 1916 and continued to serve in the Royal Navy until 1929. Born in 1902, Janet Dalgleish recalled the determination 'to get the job done' in 1914, the dislike for the Belgians, the food shortages, the fear of German prisoners of war and the hordes of wounded in Perth Royal Infirmary.

Readers interested in checking detailed sources will find them in *War and Social Change* by Dr Bill Harding in the Archive Unit at the A K Bell Library, Perth.

CONTENTS

ILLUSTRATIONS

FOREWORD

Even at this distance, the First World War is imprinted on our consciousness as a watershed of history: the end of the long sunlit Victorian afternoon of British imperial power, the first medieval war fought with weapons of mass destruction, the slaughter of an entire generation at the hands of generals better acquainted with horses than with men.

Three-quarters of a century have allowed mythology and a kind of grim romance to cloud historical truth. Ten million men may have died as a result of conflict, but the influenza pandemic which swept the world in its immediate aftermath carried off twice as many. And the eventual defeat of Germany was more the fruit of economic blockade than the unspeakable waste of life in the trenches of Flanders.

We know of the Somme and the Ypres Salient, of Vimy Ridge and Loos. We know much less of the home front, beyond a fuzzy picture of drawn blinds in bereaved streets, and men on leave too traumatised to tell their families how conditions really were in the mud of northern France. We think of it in domestic terms as the war which restricted pub hours and liberated women, the catalyst of the century's greatest social upheaval.

Dr Bill Harding tells, in meticulous detail, a different story. Taking the example of the City of Perth he not only traces the war's effects on those back home, but shows how many changes in society, so easily and conveniently ascribed to the conflict, were the result of undercurrents flowing long before the assassination at Sarajevo in 1914 triggered the cataclysm. It is a fascinating examination of how great wars can both advance and retard the march of society and can, more surprisingly, leave it remarkably undisturbed.

Alan Hamilton
The Times staff correspondent and author

First World War Shrine, St John's Kirk, Perth

INTRODUCTION

War has always had an unhealthy fascination for man, not least for those who, safe in their armchairs, have never heard the roll of drum, seen the flash of steel, or sniffed the whiff of grapeshot.

The First World War of 1914-1918 has attracted an enormous amount of comment and analysis. By 1935 alone there were over 20,000 books in print describing the conflict. The number today is vastly greater, most dealing with the glorification of war and the courage of men and women, regardless of the colour of their uniform. There are hundreds of regimental histories and thousands of accounts of personal experience. Hence, the First World War is frequently seen as a 'total war' and a watershed in history.

However interesting these accounts may be, they leave untouched important issues such as the effect of the war on society. Did class values change? Did housing improve? Did dress habits alter? Was there an increase in drinking and crime? Was there an improvement in health? Did women benefit? Did the power of the State increase? Was poverty reduced? Were trade unions encouraged? How was industry affected? The answers, however, will vary from region to region.

Perth is an excellent area for an in-depth study of such questions. It is centrally located and is partly Highland and partly Lowland. It is neither rural nor heavily industrialised and early in the century it had a manageable population of under 40,000. Besides these advantages, it had three newspapers, each with a different political outlook. Furthermore, it was a garrison town and home depot for the Black Watch. In many ways it is rather like Stirling, its sister-city and rival gateway to the Highlands. Most important of all, the local library has a splendid Archive Unit with hundreds of thousands of documents, many of which are examined in this book for the first time.

Visual sources for Perth are poor for 1910-1922. Police records show why: all photography in Perth was forbidden and every shop was searched for postcards. When found, they were systematically destroyed. The few that have survived are of little value. Most photographs, legally taken for propaganda purposes - smiling soldiers and cheering crowds - are all obviously posed.

As the impact of war can only be measured against the background of pre-war events, the framework of this study is 1910-1922.

1910-1914

Because of its central place in Scottish history, Perth has long been described as a city even though technically it is nothing more than a Royal Burgh. Not that it was ever large in terms of population or area. Indeed, in 1910, with a population hovering over the 36,000 mark it was at its highest figure ever. The increase at this point was due to the transfer, in May 1909, of parts of Burghmuir, Tulloch, Friarton and Scone, to Perth, some 3,139 acres in all. With the exception of the regular coming and going of dyers for training, the population was static.

Perth, hemmed in on the banks of the Tay, is bounded to the north and south by wide-open spaces called Inches. In 1910 there was an almost rural quality about the town. Street-traders, many of them children, were everywhere hawking their wares while the pony and trap competed with dogcarts in some of the narrow lanes. There were many horses, either diminutive ponies pulling small vans or massive stallions drawing heavy carts, and, of course, horse drinking-troughs at every corner. Then there were blacksmiths such as J Ewart in the Newrow and carriage-hirers, J Masterson for instance, in Mill Street. Sheep and pigs were daily driven through the streets to the killing-house, while bull and stallion parades were weekly events. Little Dunning Market, a medieval fair, still survived and every October it flooded the High Street with stalls to the noisy delight of gypsy hawkers and packs of dogs. Poaching was the most common crime and the Town Council's greatest worry was anthrax. Sadly, there were still no ladies' lavatories and ice-cream shops were only just losing their 'dens-of-iniquity' image. But change was coming. Trams trundled through the city pursued by clouds of cyclists and there were even a few motorcars and motorbikes. In stark contrast to its rural nature, the city had the huge North British Dye Works run by the Pullar family, who had dominated Perth, socially and politically, for the last fifty years. No other factory or industry could match their power and wealth and the 2,000 workers seemed secure and content. Perth was a city with a placid flavour, more Victorian than Edwardian.

The city's contentment was reflected in the pastimes and amusements based on the river and the Inches. Rowing clubs, some dating back to 1892, were maintained by local firms, and regattas, 'jolly boat races', were especially popular. Water carnivals were used to highlight national events, and angling clubs, using tackle bought from D B Crockart in County Place, were widely patronised. Courting couples hired rowboats in the summer evenings from D Malloch or G Dutch, while macho-stalwarts from the local swimming clubs exhibited their strength in the annual Perth-to-Dundee Swim. After all, a lady had swum it in 1906! Cricket was Perth's game. The County Cricket Club had recently done well against the West Indies and members were proud of their new Cricket Pavilion. Golf, another speciality, could be played at the Artisan Golf Club on the North Inch, the King James VI Golf Club on Moncrieff Island and the recently opened Craigie Golf Course. With Joe Anderson as the local star the city had won fame. Then there were other clubs: bowling clubs with matches against Ireland; curling clubs; Perth Tennis Club; and there was ice-skating at Hillyland. Summers especially were busy with bands and concerts on the North Inch where the Perth Silver Band played popular 1911 melodies such as 'Loch Lomond Waltz' and the two-step 'Yip-i-addy!' while children watched the antics of the pierrots from Aberdeen. Walking matches were a craze revived from previous years: 1862, 1866, 1879 and 1903, and seven men from Pullars had just recently walked to Edinburgh for a bet.

The local hero in 1910 was Mark Ali, World Long Distance Walking Champion, who, at eighty-one, was still walking fifty miles a day. Running was growing in popularity, hence the Perth Marathon, and cycling too. A good second-hand bike could be bought for 40s and even Swift, a top model costing £6s10s 0d, could be paid up at 10s a month. Horse racing on the North Inch had only stopped in 1908 and had moved to Scone and Errol. Despite growing opposition on principle, menageries were common on the South Inch: Bostock and Wombell's Royal No 1 had 'Romeo', a £900 lion-tiger hybrid. Circuses too were popular: E H Bostock's International Railroad Circus, John Swallow's International Circus, Sanger's Circus and Fossett's Circus, each stressing a star-attraction like 'The Great Scenic Railway and the Great Wobbling Airship'.

North Inch, Perth, circa 1909

Photograph courtesy of Perth Museum & Art Gallery, Perth & Kinross Council, Scotland

There were specifically working-class amusements, especially football, which had increased in popularity since the formation of the Perthshire Football League in 1884. Football could inspire great passion as was the case when St Johnstone Football Club were criticised, or enormous enthusiasm when they defeated Leith Athletic 4-3 in 1914. Five-a-side was a popular variation. Gymnastic competitions, wrestling and boxing were all popular with the dye-workers, especially the latter, because of Perth's boxing champion, J B McNeil. Pigeon racing and beekeeping were rather specialised, while the allotments of the Working Men's Garden Association on Moncrieff Island attracted the retired worker. Billiards and dominoes were not considered 'respectable' despite the fact that both had leagues and the Carlton Billiards Room in South Street was rather splendid. Vaudeville, which opened in March after the pantomime season, was very well attended, particularly for 'Bosanquet, the Human Violin' or 'George I, the most marvellous ape in the world – he can drive a car and ride a bike!' It was even possible to watch minstrels for 3d, and Harry Lauder at the King's Theatre, Dundee, for 1s 6d. Farcical comedies in Perth Theatre attracted huge crowds especially productions by Fred Karno's Company or Haldane Cricton's Company in 'a musical farce'. Indoor amusements included the 1910 craze of roller-skating. Perth had two rinks. One was the Perth Roller Skating Rink in the Dunkeld Road, where one could hire Richardson skates and glide across 15,000 square feet of rock-maple for 6d until 10 p.m. The other, the Victoria Roller Skating Rink in Victoria Street, had a cafe and music from the Fechney Boys' Band. The six teams in the Perth District Rink Hockey League held many matches throughout the year. A sunny day offered the chance of a picnic on Buckie Braes and, if it rained, a visit to Mrs Jarley's Waxworks in Bridgend Hall for 1s or Stewart's Waxworks in Scott Street for 2d.

Middle-class pastimes were more cultured. Recitals were held in St John's Kirk. There was the Perth Musical Society as well as amateur theatricals, bazaars, fêtes or 'the Berlioz method of learning French.' There were 'serious plays' at the Theatre, like *The Doll's House* and *Is Marriage a Failure*? or a powerful melodrama such as *Brought to Ruin,* one of the growing number of 'realistic plays', or the more sedate *Mikado*. There was a Perth Whist Club, and dining out at the New Royal George Hotel Restaurant had become fashionable. For the young there were Tango Tea dances with the daring Tango, New Boston or Rag. Most people, however, were content with music at home and there was a wide range of gramophones available: the Excello at 15s; the Unique at 30s; the Climax at 35s and the splendid Lord at 42s. The best homophone records were 3s each and all Perth was talking about the Cinch, 'the latest gadget, which at 52s 6d, will play anything.' A good violin could be purchased for 17s 6d, an organ for £12 10s 0d, a Bard piano for £9 10s 0d, while an upright Steinway in rosewood cost £70. Those who aspired to a higher social milieu flirted with the county gentry, visited Fine Art Exhibitions, attended Grand Opera, danced at hunt balls, usually in Edinburgh. One aristocratic sport, however, had caught the public's imagination: aeronautics. The Honourable Charles

Rolls helped organise the First Scottish International Aviation Meeting at Lanark with flights in Bleriots and JAPs and founded two flying schools. The death of Rolls at Bournemouth was much mourned in Perth where he was respected as 'a daring and enterprising experimentalist'.

For the middle class in Perth, life was very pleasant. The spate of private house building at the start of the century had largely abated and by 1910 the city was spreading west to Burghmuir and Cherrybank. Prices were reasonable: a half-villa in Tullylumb cost £835; a villa in Jeanfield cost £430 and a flat in Barossa Place, £250. Properties were easy to find. The men who lived in these areas were already moving away from strictly formal attire. In 1910, sports jackets, colourful socks and shoes were popular for relaxed dress and, even at work, silk hats and frock coats were fewer every year. Wives were still rather grand: classic hair-frames, Pompadour and Turban, beneath a Chantecler hat crowned with a pheasant. Ostrich feathers were as popular for matrons as Peter Pan collars were for young women. Colours were a riot of Old Rose, Amethyst, Sky, Peach and Gold, while furs on sale at McEwens in St John Street ranged from mole, squirrel, marmot and bear to possum. Corsetry was essential and woollen muffs and 'pigs' (foot warmers) were highly favoured. Such people liked to wear evening dress and to buy a brace of pheasants from G Stobie, game-dealer in the High Street, Havana cigars from R B Smith and Son in St John Street and claret from McDiarmid's. Their Valhalla tea, Egyptian cigarettes, turtle soup, duck and salmon, always came from P McArthur and Sons, grocers.

The working class, or classes (there were several of them) lived differently. A skilled artisan would live in a four-roomed flat in George Street at an annual rent of £9, smoke a briar pipe and drink Ragett's Nourishing Stout at 2½d a pint. He would wear a 30s ready-made suit from Stewart's tailors in the High Street, read a novel from Hampton's in Scott Street at 6d a week and occasionally snort Sandy McNab's snuff at 4d an ounce. His wife would wear a corset and knickers at 1s each with a striped, gingham underskirt at 3s 6d, all purchased through R A Storey in South Methven Street. On special occasions she would wear a feather boa and ruffle costing 18s 6d, smoke a Virginian cigarette and visit Madame Rosa, fortune-teller, in the Old Ship Inn. The unskilled, the 'underclass' in modern terms, probably lived in the Thimblerow,

Cow Vennel or Castle Gable or perhaps in the Skinnergate, Pomarium or Canal Street. There the houses were either 'unfit' or 'dangerous', often without toilets. Some 31% lived in one or two rooms, almost all of which were overcrowded.

Bad drainage and rats were so common that the *Perthshire Advertiser* declared that 'the slums of Perth are a disgrace.' But conditions were improving. The Housing and Town Planning Act 1908 had given the Town Council powers to demolish or upgrade houses by installing water-closets. At the same time Perth Trades' Council was campaigning against excessive rents and all the local political parties were urging the need for well-planned houses with low rents. The Town Council knew that the city was desperately short of decent housing and hoped that the ever-increasing legislation might carry the solution: the Housing of the Working Classes Act 1890; the Burgh Police (Scotland) Acts 1892 and 1893; the Industrial and Provident Societies Act 1893; the Small Dwellings Acquisition Act 1859 and the Housing and Town Planning Act 1909. Even though building regulations in Perth date back to 1878, there was much to be done to combat the landlord's increased powers of eviction granted by the House Letting and Rating (Scotland) Act 1911 and to extend local authority housing in Perth which was already greater than in Glasgow. The way ahead had already been shown by Pullars' model cottages at Tulloch. These had recently been praised by the Royal Commission on Housing in Scotland.

The Town Council meanwhile were involved in a host of schemes. Priority was given to sewage and water supply. New building was undertaken: a new reservoir at Burghmuir; new streets, Darnhall, Church Street and Albany Street; new schools, Craigie and Northern District; a new bridge; a new city hall and a new infirmary. There was even discussion on a new site for Perth Academy and the possibility of building a crematorium. Town Council sessions were rumbustious. Attracting new industries and more tourists was becoming more complex every year, hence the necessity of having fourteen committees by 1911 and the general use of typewriters and telephones by 1912. These new developments were financed, in the main, by profits from the city's transport system.

'Hill of the Wynd House', circa 1909

Photograph courtesy of Perth Museum & Art Gallery, Perth & Kinross Council, Scotland

In 1910, Perth had four transport lines, Scone, Cherrybank, Dunkeld Road and Craigie. Powered by horses until 1905, they had been abandoned because they lost money. Electric traction was introduced during 1905-1906, but this too soon lost money and the Town Council were faced with the question of whether or not to purchase buses. Trams had always had snags: 'Sunday Cars' irritated the godly, as did illuminated tram stops; the motormen and conductors were forever in search of a rise; horrendous accidents were common and the system involved an outlay of £75,000. The Town Council tried many solutions: displaying advertisements on trams; closing non-paying lines; and introducing return fares and season tickets. None worked. They had to buy buses. In March 1911 the city began 'a Motor Bus Trial' which was so successful that they bought two thirty-seaters, a Belhaven and a Halley. Soon, despite protests from horse-hirers, there were buses to Almondbank and Tulloch. As bus receipts rose, services were laid on to Bridge of Earn and Balbeggie. Inevitably, there were now bus accidents but, despite this, the Town Council ordered more.

It was the advent of the motorcar, however, which had the greatest impact on the city between 1910 and 1914. Many still viewed the Motor Act 1903 as a dangerous amendment of the Locomotive on Highway Act 1896 and argued that registering cars and extending speed limits from 14 mph to 20 mph was absurd. Their objections raged on for years: there would be traffic jams; horses would be frightened; roads would be ruined and rates increased. There were certainly more accidents. Horses alone killed six and injured forty-one in Perth in 1910. Others thought the motorcar a boon. New shops appeared, amongst them George Valentine's Motor Engineering Shop in South Street. Perth County Motor Garage Company in Speygate opened in 1910, Valentine's Garage in King Edward Street in 1912 and Pullars' Garage in Union Lane in 1914. The motorcar also brought problems. New streets, more signposts and notices and far more speed restrictions were now required.

A speed restriction of 10 mph imposed in central Perth did little to prevent traffic jams and to protect cyclists. Much needed traffic police appeared in September 1913. The motorcar even had an effect on road construction and technology as the Town Council realised that wider roads and better surfaces were safer. Car speed was on the increase and in July 1914 a man was found doing 42 mph on the Dundee Road. As the motorcar became more popular, new words and expressions became part of everyday language: 'speedster'; 'road hog' and 'scorching' for example. There were changes to ladies' dress as well. Ladies' motoring veils, in helio, mole and grey, were selling at 2s 11d, while a motoring coat could be had for 34s 6d. Newspapers too recognised the existence of the motorcar with the introduction of a motor column.

The popularity of the motorcar was alarming. The 1914 Commer aroused the passions of men like H S Pullar in the Auto Club at a time when a used five-seater Argyll cost £50 and a new Lagonda with 11 hp only £130. Both the motorcar and the motorbike stimulated the desire to explore the countryside and soon replaced the 19th century bicycle. Before long the newspapers were full of motor-holiday advertisements to the seaside. Naturally, there was a negative side: a whole battery of new legal offences and punishments, an 84s fine for speeding at 27 mph for example; licence frauds; racing cars on the North Inch, and lengthy debates on the legality of speed traps.

Another astonishing feature during 1910-1914 was the rapid rise of the cinema. Perth proved no exception to the cutthroat competition apparent elsewhere. Cinema, considered little more than a toy at first, soon blossomed into an elegant art form. Its impact was dramatic. In 1911, it forced the Victoria Roller-Skating Rink into bankruptcy and in 1913, the conversion of the Empire Music Hall in South Methven Street into the Empire Picture House. Patrons soon objected to the 'lack of class' image, and the desire for a more sophisticated ambience saw new rough-and-ready cinemas, like the Electric Theatre in Alexandra Street, go to the wall. By 1913, Perth had five cinemas: the BB (Bright and Beautiful) Picture House in Victoria Street, the Corona Picture House in the High Street, the La Scala in Scott Street, the King's Cinema in South Methven Street and the City Hall. They offered a wide fare. In January 1914 the BB Picture House showed *Riddle of the Tin Soldier* from Monday to Wednesday and *Our New Minister* from Thursday to Saturday. As filmmaking was a speculative area, it attracted many companies which soon had huge circuits distributing a vast range of film topics. There was no lack of innovation. In February 1914, Perth showed

The Dictator, an 'éclair-coloured drama' followed in April 1914 by Kinnecolour. Interval entertainment still consisted of 'banjo-dances' as was the case at La Scala in July 1914 when *The Curse of War* was shown. As in everything else, fads emerged. For example, in 1913, there were sacred films while 'immoral films' (as determined by the Film Board) were completely ignored. With constant improvements demanded by a visually hungry public, it was only a question of time before Biocolour, Chronophone, Filaphone, Vivaphone and Cinephone would be surpassed.

One aspect of pre-war society was changing almost imperceptibly - the press. Perth was fortunate in that her three newspapers covered the spectrum of political belief. The *Perth Courier* was a long established liberal publication, while the *Constitutional* was an equally respectable unionist product. Both argued the great issues of the day, the former supporting Free Trade for example, and the latter, Protectionism. Fortunately, there was also a middle-of-the-road liberal-unionist newspaper, the *Perthshire Advertiser*, which tended to be more moderate, more objective and less partisan. All were changing, however, due to the need to win a mass-market through better technology. Photographs first appeared in June 1912 with pictures of Pullars' strikers and by 1913 they had replaced the old-style, front-page cartoons. Varying the price, as the *Perthshire Advertiser* did, 1d on Wednesday and ½d on Saturday, was another technique introduced to win readers. The *Perth Courier* responded by bringing out a 3 p.m edition on Tuesdays for 1d.

Language was changing too. The heavy, pedantic, 19th century prose, with such expressions as 'ozone dipsomaniacs' for 'people on the beach' was being replaced by a sharper, shorter, more dramatic version and 'excursionists' now became 'trippers.' The emergence of a national slang with words like 'flapper' marks the decline of old, regional dialects and the growing influence of the film. The florid nature of descriptions was also disappearing. 'Gay cavaliers' and 'pretty weddings' were already old-fashioned by 1910. Of even greater importance was the now sustained concentration on sensation and scandal stripped of verbiage. Thus, divorce cases gave more intimate details of adultery and murder trial reports used fewer asterisks.

Headlines such as 'Lancashire Pit Disaster' or 'Fear of Ulster Civil War' were in bigger print to imply greater threat. Advertisements too, as old as time as they might be, now had a no-holds-barred outspokenness: 'Clarks B41 pills for discharges from urinary organs.' Commercial psychology was even more blatant: 'Eat Plainsman Oats and drink Cocoa as used by the Royal Family!'

The very format of the newspapers revealed a changing world. Film reviews, pollution reports, 'Suffrage News from Abroad' and serials began to push book reviews, garden notes, football features and sports news to the back pages, and regular items, such as Presbytery, Town Council and School Board reports were reduced to summaries. Being provincial newspapers, they were less interested in the Mad Mullah in British Somaliland than in the fact that several local people were killed in the San Francisco Earthquake or lost with the Titanic.

Another change was coming: newsreels. The funeral of Sir Robert Pullar in September 1912 was caught on 300 feet of cinematograph film at a cost of £10, while H S Pullar returned from his African safari in January 1914 with 6,000 feet of film entitled, *Big Game Hunting.*

Some problems, of course, never change. Throughout the 19th century, drink was the root of the social malaise in Perth and it had barely improved by 1910. There were ninety-five registered drinking *howffs* in the city and drink was cheap by any standard. For instance, Schiehallion Old Scotch was only 4s a bottle while McIntosh's No 2 special was just 3s. It was even possible to buy two bottles of whisky and two of port for a mere 10s 6d from Matthew Gloag's Wine and Spirit Merchants, Kinnoull Street. The pubs in the centre of the city: Old Ship Inn; Stormont Arms; Britannia Inn; Glencoe; Empire and Bee Bar were ghastly drinking dens, each with a long history of drunken violence. Statistics show that 73% of all crime in 1910-1914 was drink-related, and that drunken females were the greatest problem for the police. But drink was far from being a solely urban matter as riots at Ballinluig, Birnam, Pitlochry and Alyth clearly show. Fortunately there were many agencies pledged to fight the demon drink. The Perth Prohibition Party, the Scottish Temperance and Social Reform Association, the 'Catch-My-Pal' Movement from Ulster, temperance lectures in schools and even a TT steamer on the Tay all played their part. While there was progress, with arrests for drunkenness steadily falling from 385 in 1903, to 357 in 1908, to 203 in 1909, it was nevertheless an uphill task as even police and firemen could be found drunk on duty.

Another side of the coin was immorality. In 1913, Perth had at least twenty-four full-time prostitutes, while prostitution at the time was listed as 'an occupation'. So sordid was the seamy side of Perth nightlife that the Town Council hired night patrols for the parks.

Fortunately, murder and rape were rare, and the bulk of police work involved poaching, drunkenness, petty theft and wife assault. Police had to tackle sheep stealing, child neglect, breach of the peace, malicious damage, assaults and occasionally, fraud, photo conmen, safe robbery and 'spurious coin circulation'. Sentences were generally savage: six years' penal servitude for burglary; fourteen days for stealing a bicycle; a fine of 7s 10½d for rail trespass and 20s for reckless cycling.

Although the uniformed officer was a figure of authority there was an enormous amount of juvenile crime in 1910. Young people vandalised, stole bicycles, threw stones at trains and telephone insulators and there were minor offences such as Saturday football on the North Inch, stealing fruit and street-trading. Gangs were common and most of the members were either illegitimate or from broken homes. Punishments were much less severe than formerly, at least since the Probation of Offenders Act 1907, and no children were whipped in Perth during the 1910-1914 period. Very bad behaviour was still punished by a spell in a Reformatory or an Industrial School. Police statistics show that juvenile misbehaviour came in waves: football violence in 1906; vandalising on the South Inch in 1907; damaging trees in 1908; breaking windows in 1909; stoning trains in 1911; uprooting trees in 1913 and damaging post-boxes in 1914.

From 1903 onwards, Perth's forty-two policemen typed all their reports. They used fingerprints from 1913 and photos from London CID from 1914. Unfortunately, they usually lost their best men to the Metropolitan Police or to Canada. Each year paperwork increased due to the Motorcar Act 1903, the Shop Hours Act 1904, the Dogs Order 1906, the Children's Act 1908, the OAP Act 1908, the Housing and Town

Planning Act 1909, the Shops Act 1912 and the Mental Deficiency (Scotland) Act 1913. Consequently, the police wanted an eight-hour day, subsidised accommodation and an increase to their £96 per annum pay.

Their private files show that they spent much of their time analysing the reasons for the existence of problem families like the Quinns, Foyles and Foleys and whether habitual offenders were the product of heredity factors or environment. They set up 'criminal profiles' and established that thieves were generally small, the violent were taller, fraudsters older and most criminals had no fixed abode. They noted that many offenders were mentally ill and that each year brought new types of crime, such as the theft of National Insurance cards in 1911. They also observed that crime statistics were poor guides dependent upon one's definition of a 'crime' and they further predicted that there would be a steady rise in crimes against the person from 1907.

As for health, infant mortality fell steadily from 129.7 per 1,000 in 1889 to 83.5 per 1,000 in 1910. Much of this was due to the Perth Day Nursery Association which was founded in 1909. They were able to report the lowest birth rate ever in June 1914. This they associated with a general raising of the standard of comfort. Illegitimacy was steady at 7% but was slowly losing its stigma. For instance, birth certificates no longer stated 'birth in prison', but 'birth in an institution'. Already there was a feeling that day nurseries were indispensable. Sadly, working-class school children tended to have a catalogue of defects. At least 20% had bad teeth, skin diseases and poor speech, while an unfortunate few did not even have footwear. The School Board strove to do its best. A school nurse was appointed, free toothbrushes and boots were distributed, hygiene was taught, swimming encouraged, diets (based on cod-liver oil and Parish's syrup) were prescribed, free spectacles issued, a cooking depot opened, special classes set up for the backward and a summer holiday home established for the needy at Pitlochry. Many of these developments sprang from the Education Act 1908 which stated 'that the School Board has to feed and clothe the necessitous.' It was becoming obvious that, in the future, the State would have to pay for the needy.

Newspapers played their part with health campaigns urging more exercise, the use of 'pure milk and butter' and the need to become health conscious. Middle class Perth citizens already spent large sums on health foods such as Maltona beef, Abdine fruit drink, Vi cocoa 'for energy' and Tonol, 'the perfect tonic for the brain!' There was a cure for everything. There was Chlorodyne for bronchitis and asthma, Zambuck for piles, Peps for whooping cough and Bay Rum for baldness. Every summer, members of the middle class spent holidays in Strathpeffer, the Isle of Man or Portobello where they took pictures with 3s Pocket Kodaks. No wonder the *Perthshire Advertiser* could boast that Perth was a healthy city. Unfortunately, that was not true. Tuberculosis was rising fast, especially among the pauper class, and the appointment of a TB officer in 1912 showed that the Town Council suspected that the 'consumption scourge' could only get worse.

Believing that there were healthier climates elsewhere, many of the young emigrated. Canada was the most popular destination as reports of high wages were published almost weekly in the press. The call of the west lured at least 350 Perth people in the year 1909-1910. The flow increased when Barlas and Edwards, shipping agents, in the High Street, ran a series of 'cinematograph views' in local halls and gave talks on 'Free Land', 'The Children's Emigration Scheme', 'The Canadian Pacific Railway' and 'The Canadian Government's Appeal for Women as Wives.' But the greatest drain on Perth came in January 1913 when a new dyeing industry opened in Montreal. Over one hundred dyers left with their families and more followed in 1914 during the trade union disputes in Perth. Then, in July 1914, emigration came to an abrupt stop: there was unemployment in Canada. Australia was less popular because it wanted farm-workers rather than tradesmen. However, lectures on 'Australia's Wide Spaces' generated an emigration boom in 1910 with large numbers of young people heading for New South Wales and West Australia in particular.

The result of this movement of people was a strengthening of feeling for the Empire and this was shown in many ways. There were 'Festivals of the Empire', 'Sons of the Empire' dinners, 'News of the Empire' columns in the press and a steady stream of letters and reports. It even deepened the mystical love of one's own country, idealising valour and chivalry and seeing the UK as rural rather than industrial.

This was to prove the motivating force behind the volunteers of August 1914.

Religion, however, was changing. While the middle class saw it as 'respectability', it either meant 'evangelical rebirth' or nothing at all to the working class. Perceptive commentators had already noted the spread of atheism as well as spiritualism, theosophy and vegetarianism. As ever, superstition was not far behind.

Politics were also changing. Perth had long been a Liberal-dominated city with a list of Liberal election wins: 1885; 1886; 1895; 1900; 1906 and 1907. The two General Elections of 1910 simply continued the trend. Hence, Sir Robert Pullar, Peter Campbell and James Coates, and all other leading businessmen were members of the Perth Liberal Club in George Street. They favoured votes for women and home rule just as much as they despised the House of Lords and Protectionism. The Unionists, last in power in 1892, appeared to have little chance, but this was not so. There was a split in the Pullar family. H S Pullar became a leading Unionist, warning that Free Trade was disastrous because of the dominance of Germany. It was, however, the wave of deep and passionate feeling over Ulster that had re-invigorated the Unionists. Headlines such as 'Will There be Civil War?' and 'Revolution in Ireland' filled the average Perth reader with horror.

Socialism seemed to be making progress with the formation of a Perth Labour Party in 1907, four years before the formation of a Labour Party in Glasgow. Before long, it was well-entrenched in Perth with meetings regularly well-attended. Soon, the Party had a member on the School Board and invited prominent speakers to come to Perth. Amongst them were Will Crooks, Sidney Webb and James O'Grady. Not long after Dundee had won its first Labour MP, a call went out for a prospective parliamentary candidate for Labour in Perth. Their platform was appealing: 'We need Socialism for milk and medicine for children.' Slums and high rents were condemned and nationalised railways were demanded. Early in 1914, they even challenged the Church: 'What has the Christian Church been doing for almost 2,000 years in regard to … drink, black slavery, white slavery, housing, sweating … nothing!' The New Labour Rooms in Atholl Street were a hotbed for radical ideas. Then, in July 1912, the Dyers' Union firmly declared themselves opposed to both Socialism and Syndicalism. It was clear that until the Labour Party could win over the trade unions they would get nowhere.

George Street, 1930

The position of women was changing rapidly in the period 1910-1914. The first woman pensioner, Maggie Trotter, had just completed a fifty-year stint at Pullars' Dyeworks, while lady typists were in demand in every city office. There was already a female probation officer, a City Hall caretaker, a swimming teacher and teams of lady gymnasts. There was even mixed bathing on the Tay! The male perception of women was changing. Women were standing for school boards, suing for divorce and one had even looped the loop in a plane. The changing role of women gave rise to press articles questioning whether women could be company directors, if there would soon be women police and why women were underpaid. But some women were impatient for change and thought that the franchise was the key. They were to have a long history.

However, their first rallies and demonstrations began in Perth in 1906. But it was the opening of a branch of the WFL, the Women's Federation League, which introduced a more radical, fiery element in 1908. Their speakers were very persuasive and at a Guild Hall debate in November 1908, a motion on 'Votes for Women' was carried by sixty-one to fifty. It got no further, however, and by 1909 they were turning militant and violent, so much so, that an Anti-Suffrage League was formed. The result was that when the Lord Advocate visited Perth in January 1910, he had to have police protection. A more peaceful balance was achieved when the National Union of Women's Suffrage Societies, NUWSS, opened in Bridgend and launched a series of guest speakers: Dr Elsie Inglis; Mrs Philip Snowden and Miss Haldane of Cloan. Their non-violent policy of garden parties, rallies and cake and candy stalls was very popular in Perth where it won the support of the Town Council. A F Whyte MP even went so far as to venture his backing for equal pay. Many praised the suffragettes for their 'moderate and sensible actions in Perth', but the editor of the *Perth Courier* warned that 'The giving of an inch to the advocates of votes for women has evolved clamour for the proverbial ell.' He also posed an interesting point: 'Why are women so apathetic in municipal elections and yet so strident for the franchise?'

Perhaps in response to this rhetorical question, the NUWSS put forward candidates for the School Board elections in 1911. What demonstrations they had were conducted with lively decorum. In 1912 violence erupted in other parts of the country. Windows were smashed, there was arson, and acid was placed in post-boxes, and although it was quiet in Perth, these incidents lost the suffragettes the support of Perth Town Council. Disorder came to Perth in April 1913 with the burning of Perth Cricket Pavilion at a cost of £1,200. This was followed by a riot three days later. There were arguments for banning open-air meetings and counter-arguments on the sanctity of free speech. Then, with repeated noisy demonstrations, the police were forced to patrol public buildings at night in pairs. But it was the death of Emily Davidson in June 1913 that sparked off a torrent of emotion and four serious near-riots in Perth, leading the police to finger-print suspected arsonists.

By August the suffragettes had introduced a new ploy of chanting in churches. This was to lose them the support of the local clergy and in October there were huge Anti-Suffrage rallies in the city. The year 1913 ended with society terrified of arson and the police hot on the trail of a Miriam Pratt and a Rachel Peace whose photographs were displayed in Perth.

The police suspected that 1914 would be 'the year of crisis' and they were right. As the NUWSS broadsheet, *Common Cause*, flooded the city, the local Women's Liberal Association declared opposition to its aims. This inflamed NUWSS activists and they demanded 'more militancy now!' Arson attacks increased and in one night, 3 February 1914, three Perthshire mansions, the House of Ross, Aberuchill and St Fillans' castles, were torched, earning the fierce condemnation of the Presbytery of Perth. As might have been expected this provoked open war between militants and non-militants, while the Liverpool CID sent forty-eight photographs of 'the most wanted suspects' to Perth and issued warrants for their arrest. By June, local detectives were patrolling the grounds of Perth Royal Infirmary, while uniformed colleagues arrested suffragette speakers at the High Street Port. Then came July, a month in which the suffragettes had promised 'a lively reception' for George V and Queen Mary on their visit to Perth to open the new infirmary. Their reason was that one of their number, Miss Arabella Scott, was being forcibly fed at Perth Penitentiary. To emphasise the point they interrupted services at St Stephen's United Free Church with chants of 'O Lord, hasten the liberation of our sisters in prison,' and on 11 July, in County Place, they flung leaflets at the King as he passed in an open car. For this 'outrage', Mrs Elizabeth Crawford, aged twenty-six, was sentenced to fifteen days in prison. This provoked 'a suffragette invasion' as pickets paraded nightly outside the jail. Next day, 300 women marched to the penitentiary gates to join some 2,000 in a protest against forcible feeding, while six dedicated activists entered St John's Kirk East and commenced chanting.

When news of such incidents reached London, questions were asked in the House of Commons. The authorities were persuaded to release some of the detainees because of public disquiet. Over the next few days, St Ninian's Cathedral was visited twice by activists, causing the Cathedral Provost to remark: 'I must confess that I admire the pluck and determination of the militants.' With interruptions to the film show in the La Scala, and deputations from the public against 'the Botany Bay in Perth', it only took a mass rally on the North Inch by Perth and District Trades and Labour Council for the authorities to yield: Miss Arabella Scott was released. She and her colleagues had destroyed £97,975 worth of property in Scotland.

Behind all this political turmoil, economic forces moved on relentlessly and to the amazement of most people, in August 1911, there was a sudden rise in food prices. Sugar rose by ½d, bacon by 1d and a loaf by ½d to 6½d. The *Perth Courier* announced the return of 'hard times'.

The Board of Trade was naturally concerned. In 1913 it published a report which claimed that Perth was the most costly place to live in the UK. If prices in London were taken as 100, prices in Glasgow would be 99, Aberdeen 101, Edinburgh 103, Dundee 104 and Perth 108. In other words, prices in Perth had risen 16%. It was further disclosed that this upward trend had started in 1906 and by 1913, rent, food, fuel and clothing had gone up 10%, but wages had only risen 6% in Aberdeen, 5% in Dundee, 4% in Glasgow, 3% in Edinburgh and Perth. As for meat, prices were up 9% in Glasgow, 13% in Edinburgh, 16% in Dundee, 20% in Perth and 25% in Aberdeen. Rents had also risen in Edinburgh and Dundee by 10% and in Aberdeen, Glasgow and Perth by 13%. It was obvious that poverty would increase too and that industrial trouble was just around the corner. By 1914 the average wage was 25s 8d per week, while the average outlay on food was 23s 9d per week. There was a realisation that if there was war, food prices would rise.

Poverty was not new. On the contrary, it had always been a problem in Scottish urban history. In 1910, however, it increased. The Perth Medical Officer observed in October 1909 that despite fifteen degrees of frost, a large number of children were attending school barefooted and that many were undersized and under-nourished. Yet there were no fewer than thirty-seven agencies in the city designed to fight poverty, all non-partisan and all non-sectarian. Among these were Hillside Homes, founded in 1878, Sick Poor Nursing Society (1885) and Perth Hospice (1910).

Despite effort and expenditure, there seemed no solution to the city's poverty. Some proposed introducing a Civic Guild as well as soup kitchens. The *Perthshire Advertiser* observed that Perth Prison fuelled the problem with an annual discharge of 239 ex-convicts, most of whom just stayed in the city. The realisation that the very poor were carriers of TB led to meetings to discuss the matter and to extend poor relief. Analysis led to a startling headline on 23 October 1911 in the *Perthshire Advertiser*: 'Poverty and Disease are Rampant in Perth'. Confirmation lay in the fact that 701 had applied for relief and the number of licensed city pawnbrokers such as Jacob Samuel and Jane Cohen, of which there were eighteen in 1913. Another benchmark was the number of debt cases appearing monthly in the Sheriff Court, a total of seventy-four in January 1914. While Perth tried hard to return any vagrant to his or her place of birth by legal means, the Dean of Guild denounced 'the thriftless class that menace the State.' Perth, however, had its attraction for the county's 414 professional tramps. In 1914 there were four dosshouses, one of which, Skinnergate Model, had 19,145 clients in 1913 alone. The city refused to entertain such numbers and in July 1914 reduced the poor rate by 1d.

The years 1910-1914 saw a strenuous effort being made by the trade unions to get a hold in Perth. In 1910, they succeeded with the Municipal Employees' Association and the Perth Shop Assistants' Union, but failed with the Upholsterers' Union. When town employees agitated for a week's holiday with pay, they were granted it. Having heard how girls in Perth had been victimised for trying to form a trade union, the Scottish Trades Union Congress, meeting in Dundee in April 1911, decided to launch a crusade. They nominated four of their best people: Alderman Hayhurst of the Amalgamated Society of Dyers and Cleaners; George Dallas (close friend of Jimmy Maxton) with his wife, Agnes Brown, of the National Federation of Women Workers and Mary MacArthur, also of the NFWW, to attend meetings in the Independent Labour Party Rooms in Atholl Street. There they stated their aims of achieving higher wages, shorter hours and better conditions for all. They immediately formed a Dyers' Union. The two women, enlisted by Miss McLean, a NFWW organiser, soon had 400 members in the Wallace Works alone.

Then in August 1911, the Great Rail Strike completely paralysed the Perth region. The *Perthshire Advertiser* gave its verdict on 28 August: 'Great Victory for Trade Unionism - Strikers Win!' The effectiveness of a concerted strike action was plain for all to see and every section in the community took up arms. The printers, members of the Typographical Society, demanded a closed shop and an end to 'female dilution'. They had little support from the city because of their 1900 strike record when they had used violence and intimidation which had resulted in imprisonment for some of them. They had already been granted a 1s rise and a reduction in the working week in 1908 and many felt that with 31s a week they had enough. This infuriated the printers and they started a '34s for 50 hours' campaign based on the increased cost of living. The Perth and District Trades' Council were worried about the possibility of renewed violence. A F Whyte MP stated that troops could only be used if the community was 'violently blackmailed'. Those who did not belong to strong trade unions had no chance. These would have included typists who only earned £26 per annum, the scavengers, carters and gas depot labourers. The latter only had 22s for a fifty-one hour week and they were granted a rise of 1s 6d. However, when they asked for more they were refused and were told that their work was easier as a result of the introduction of mechanical stocking.

In 1912, coal rose by 1s 6d to 1s 9d a cwt and the *Perthshire Advertiser* asked: 'Is the country mad? The coal strike, menacing and injurious as it is, is merely a symptom of the volcanic unrest which seems to permeate the crust of practically every branch of labour in this country. What is the cause of it? Is the country ripe for an Industrial Revolution? Are the workers so downtrodden that they are prepared to resort to desperate methods to enforce their demands?' The sudden news that the NFWW was now the biggest trade union in the city came as an unpleasant shock to employers. It seemed to inspire the joiners, who with 8d an hour, were furious to learn that 9½d was the rate in Dundee and they threatened to strike as they had done in 1900 and 1901. They did so - and won ½d.

Bakers wanted 2s and the painters, who had a record of strikes in 1900 and 1906 as well as 'violent intimidation', demanded a rise too. Then, just as the public learned that there were now 120 in the shop

Assistants' Union, the police demand for 'minor adjustments' to their salaries was granted.

In January 1913, the painters delivered their demands. They wanted a half-day on Saturdays, double time for working on public holidays, 2d a day extra when working outside the city, a week's holiday at midsummer and if working then, time and a half, and 2s for apprentices. Despite having pickets at the railway station, non-union labour managed to enter the city and the strike collapsed. However, the masters awarded ½d. The union responded by asking for another 1d. The power of the strike was then demonstrated by the plumbers who asked for 1d extra. They were offered an immediate payment of ½d and a further ½d to be paid later. This they refused. When they were then given 1d increase, they instantly asked for yet another 1d.

This was the signal for the March 1913 wage-scramble in Perth. The plasterers requested 1d and were given ½d; the tailors were promised ½d within a year; the drovers wanted 1s 6d per week; the glaziers received ½d per day; the bakers, 2s per week; and the blacksmiths were granted a fifty-one hour week. The unrest spread. Two hundred came out at Stanley Mill where the average female wage was only 12s a week; the workers at Invergowrie Paper Works went on strike for an extra 2s and a train-load of unemployed men from Perth and Dundee who were sent to Leith to break a stevedore strike, were violently attacked. Everywhere there was unrest. In Perth in 1914, the water workers demanded a rise as did the road labourers and the police, while the tailors refused to wait any longer for their increase. Not all were successful. The joiners were refused, as were the gas and general workers, but significantly, railwaymen were now asking for a minimum wage and the carters had set up a union.

None of the above seemed likely to affect the big mills and factories of Perth. After all, labour was cheap in the city and what unemployment there was, was usually short and irregular. The causes of unemployment, however, were still a mystery, despite the existence of Labour Exchanges. The city was conscious of its growing wealth as rates income continued to rise and investments in Canada and tea flourished. There was even £1,500,000 in the County and Perth Savings Bank. Trade unionists were infuriated to learn that over a million of it was owned by the city's six leading industrialists. Throughout 1910, the North British Dye Works, owned by the Pullar family, felt secure. After all, they had just set up a joint stock company, John Pullar and Sons Ltd, Dyers and Cleaners, under the Companies (Consolidated) Act 1908 which was valued at £200,000.

Everything seemed fine until the coal and rail strike of March 1912. Soon 2,500 were idle. After this devastating blow, recovery was slow. Unfortunately, the Dyers' Union seized this moment to demand higher wages and better conditions. When rises, which since 1882 were virtually automatic annually on 1 June, were announced by Pullars, the union, with only 200 members (but a fighting fund of £50,000) denounced 'the miserable wage of 22s after a long, seven years' apprenticeship, the lack of an established scale and poor overtime payments.' The management foolishly did not explain the significance of a limited liability company or the effects of the National Insurance Act and especially the fact that the financial year now began in November. A deputation from the Finishing Department was rebuffed and a rumour spread that the delegation would be sacked. Some 240 from the Glazing Department went on strike and were immediately locked-out. Pickets were set up and demands were lodged for a wage scale: 6s at fourteen years and 30s at thirty years. More rumours spread and 200 from the Ironing Department walked out, led by Councillor Stewart from Dundee who had come to organise them. George Dallas, wired the Dyers' Union Headquarters in Bradford for help. The *Perth Courier* had no doubt but that the blame lay with 'management insensitivity.'

On 4 June 1912, the strikers gathered on the North Inch and marched through the city, while the Trades' Council set up a strike fund. Fear of management reprisals, especially against those in tied houses, spread rapidly even though the firm declared that nobody would be sacked and nobody would be victimised. R D Pullar gave a small rise to the apprentices and announced that other workers would be considered in November, while he told the press that 'Trade union organisers are pouring into Perth from all over.' He was right. Miss McIntosh and William Rushworth had arrived to add their organisational skills to the strike. This did not go unnoticed. The *Perthshire Advertiser* commented:

'It is rather singular, not to say ominous, that with the inception of trade unions among the dye-workers, a strike should instantly follow.' R D Pullar added his view: 'We don't pay off in slack spells and the female workers are animated because of the suffragettes and the NFWW.' It was certainly true that only one male dyer was on strike.

At this point the strikers' solidarity began to crack and the 500 involved blamed the dyers who were trying to widen differentials. The union called a vote, but only 201 voted and of these just fifty wanted to carry on. They went back to work. Wisely, management did not gloat despite the fact that the general public were bitterly opposed to the union. But that very night of defeat, 500 more women joined the NFWW. The *Perthshire Advertiser*'s headline: 'Trade Union Defeated', merely encouraged the Dyers' Union to greater effort. Then the management made a tactical error: they announced the lapse of the Sickness Benefit Society (because of the National Insurance Act), and stated that the summer break would have to be cut to make up for lost production. It seemed like spiteful revenge and some union activists quit for Canada. Yet a few months later the firm granted the dyers a scale of 24s at twenty years of age and 34s at twenty-eight.

A lull followed during which time the firm installed generators and bought vans. The *Constitutional* reflected on how long it would be before there would be a Labour MP in Perth 'as workers abandon Liberalism and move left.' In September 1913, the Dyers' Union renewed their attack by demanding a national minimum wage of 36s plus 2s 'for all', a fifty-one hour week, and time and a half overtime. This was clearly an impossible demand, but Rushworth cleverly chose this moment to declare his belief in votes for women and equal pay. 'Why should a man have 31s and a woman only 11s?' he queried. As a result more women joined the union. In March 1914, the union again changed tactics and sent its shop stewards to ask for a rise. R D Pullar was annoyed by this and despite the fact that the union now had over 600 members, he suggested that if they were dissatisfied they should go. While the press screamed 'Strife!' Rushworth shouted, 'Victimisation!' But it was the *Perthshire Advertiser* that caught the mood by stating that there was a feeling of fear in the Works.

Eventually twenty-seven workers were asked to leave and twenty-six of them were leading unionists. R D Pullar denied that he was trying to smash the union, but few believed him, especially when it was learned that he had replaced the men who left with boys. Obviously his motives were to lower production costs, to pay for the recent wage increases and to crush the trade union. The management, deeply annoyed, asked its workforce to sign a Petition of Loyalty. Eighty per cent (1,671) did so and twenty per cent (276) refused. This marked the end of an era.

P and P Campbell, Perth Dye Works, invested heavily in new machinery in the years 1910-1914. Like Pullars they had formed a Limited Liability Company in 1912, but the March 1912 coal and rail strike shattered their confidence in the railways and made them realise that 'dyeing was no longer a prosperous trade.' This was a view shared by Thomson's Fair City Dyeworks and they slowly withdrew from dyeing to concentrate on laundry work which they found highly profitable. Coates' Balhousie Works found that jute costs had risen steadily since 1910, while the 1912 strike had left them without coal. Carpet yarn shot up in price in 1913, while workers were given rises amounting to 12½%.

Shields' Wallace Works found their profits soaring in 1910 despite rising costs and worry over US tariffs. But the 1912 strike put them on short time. This was followed by a weavers' request for a cut in hours without loss of pay. Nevertheless 1911 was a good year and big extensions in the plant were planned. Then the announcement that the 1912 profit was £11,444 proved to be 'a signal for unrest.' Miss Sloan of the NFWW demanded a 10% rise on the basis that 'Perth has the highest food costs and lowest pay.' She had a strong case: the workers had had no real rise since 1893, just 'adjustments, reductions and restorations', but now 80% of the women were in the union and they wanted more: better yarn; 2s immediately; 10% on piece-rates; equal division of work; pay at time-rate while waiting; towels; and cups. All they received were the towels! HG Shields tried to wriggle out of any commitment by accusing the weavers of 'being careless and costing the firm some £3,000 a year.' The union replied that weavers often had to look after five looms each. A strike ballot showed that 332 wanted to stop work and only fifty-seven voted to continue. Miss Sloan emphasised their motives: 'Perth is very dear and since 1906 the value of 20s has fallen to 16s 8d, and eggs, bacon and butter are dearer.' She warned her members to have 'no fighting with blacklegs!' The male workers now called in Rushworth and he declared a strike from 23 September 1913 and demanded that strikers receive 7s a week. H G Shields thundered that 'the trade unions are making 800 idle!' and then settled the matter quietly with a 5% rise and the formation of a committee of twelve to meet monthly with management. H G Shields had learned a lesson - the value of solidarity - and he appealed to fellow-industrialists to form a Federation of Employers 'to match the Unions.' As many expected, the firm's profits for 1913 were a miserable £5,420 'due to higher wages and taxes as well as the large reduction in the US tariff.'

The economic health of the other city employers varied. Moncrieff Glass Works declared that March 1912 'had nearly killed trade', a view shared by Garvie and Deas, Dyers, South Methven Street, which almost closed down. The Co-operative in Perth was unpopular, and the General Accident Insurance Company, John Douglas and Sons, as well as Scone Preserve Works were all having shareholder problems. Only the Perthshire Laundry Company Limited, St Catherine's Road, the Hamilton Steam Laundry, Dunkeld Road and the Scone Laundry Company Limited, were really thriving, that is, of course, apart from John Dewar and Sons Limited, whose whisky profits were a massive £152,762. At the harbour, coastal trade with London, Leith, Dundee and Newcastle brought in a steady flow of glass, manure, salt and potatoes, while the foreign trade with Hamburg, Riga, St Petersburg, Archangel and Ghent brought in wood, oilcake, cement, maize, ice and slates. But even these had an element of risk: the river tended to drop in summer and ships were easily stranded.

Despite the foreign trade, foreigners were not popular in Perth. There was an unfounded belief that Russian ships brought cholera, while Italians were openly disliked. By 1910 there were eighteen Italian families in the city including Cura, Giulanotti, Manattini and Giacopazzi. They had all prospered, eight were confectioners, six were fish restaurateurs and four were grocers.

The largest alien group in Perth were the Germans among whom were the Buhrer, Nef, Kumerer, and Liebow families. They formed a congregation of 100 in the West Hall, St John's Parish, under their Pastor, Herr E Albrecht. Their presence was strongly felt: the shops were full of Hochheimer, Zeller and Moselle wines at 1s 2d a bottle, Bechstein pianos at £85 and Blickensdorf typewriters. German lessons were held in the Temperance Hall and the Berlin Meister Orchestra under Herr Blane played in the Lesser City Hall. But, there was growing resentment over trade. After all, Germany favoured Protection and the UK Free Trade. Besides, there was great envy of Germany's commercial success. There was even a feeling of inferiority with Perth dyers having to go to Germany to learn the latest techniques. Then there was the fame of their achievements in teaching, technology, music and science.

But it was the psychological effect of fear that sowed distrust. The hysterical idea in 1903 that the Germans were planning an attack on the Forth Bridge sparked off war novels like *The Riddle of the Sands* by Erskine Childers and *The Thirty-Nine Steps* by John Buchan. News that Germany was expanding her fleet simply confirmed suspicions. Although there were denials from officialdom, behind the scenes it was different. In January 1914, Major Kell of the War Office wrote to the Chief Constable warning him of 'aliens and espionage'. More and more evidence seemed to indicate that war was coming: the huge extensions to Krupps' Armament Works; the Bruno Langer flying feat of fourteen hours in the air; the notorious Kiel Naval Dinner for Prince Henry of Prussia and the news that the cruiser *Seydlitz* could travel at twenty-eights knots. But did these all add up to war? Surely war was inconceivable in the year 1914?

Corner of High Street and Meal Vennel, circa 1924

Photograph courtesy of Perth Museum & Art Gallery, Perth & Kinross Council, Scotland

1914

The casual reader of the *Perth Courier* on Tuesday, 4 August 1914 might well have missed the insignificant paragraph informing the public that the country was now involved in 'a dreadful war'. This is not surprising. After all, the headlines were more important: 'Sewage Scheme to Cost £250,000!' and 'Football Sensation - T Paxton, Half-back Signed by Cowdenbeath Rather than Perth!' Even 'Random Notes', a column specifically designed to keep readers abreast of foreign affairs, made no mention of the impending conflict on the Continent. Indeed, in terms of inked space, the Errol Races, the problem of Scottish Home Rule and the Sweat Pea Exhibition in the City Hall commanded greater attention. Next day, the *Constitutional* and *Perthshire Advertiser* were both equally restrained: 'Britain at War!' Not that the editors were obtuse. The Sarajevo Incident had after all taken place as far back as 28 June and seemed to be solely a Balkan matter. Again, there had been a spate of assassinations over the previous decade and none of these had had serious repercussions for this country. Consequently, it took almost a week before Perth's editors realised that the war was to be 'The Great European War!'

The general public could not comprehend how Britain could possibly be involved and were anxious to hear the views of local dignitaries. A few were hawks. F Norie-Miller of Cleeve declared, 'We must fight now!' and Lord Dean of Guild Brown was adamant that 'The Germans are asking for it.' The majority showed reluctance, with the Earl of Kinnoull of Balhousie Castle conceding that, 'It is our responsibility,' A F Whyte MP, 'It was inevitable,' Sir John A Dewar MP, 'We can't avoid it,' and the Rev P R Landreth, 'We must stand by our obligations.' A few, such as A Wilkie MP and A W Ponsonby MP urged neutrality, while some, like Harry G Shields, warned of the cost. 'It will threaten our Russian flax supplies and could kill the linen industry' he announced. Most citizens seemed to agree with the London opinion that 'the war might well be localised as the Balkans don't concern us. However, we must not support Russia.'

There was no indecision on the part of the military. Reservists and members of the Territorial Army had long suspected that they would be needed in Ireland and they were quick to respond to the call for mobilisation. Within hours they were assembling at the Barracks or the Drill Hall in Tay Street with the 6th Black Watch or the Army Service Corps. Although the activity was described as 'stirring' and even 'feverish', there were no signs in Perth according to the *Perth Courier* of 'that senseless form of patriotic imbecility known as *mafficking.*' Soon, as the city was designated a War Station, thousands of troops were making their way to Perth. When the North and South Inches became training areas for drilling and trench digging, it was announced that an expanded Army Pay Corps would be based in Perth which was also to become a major Territorial Army Centre. The Barracks was quickly extended and the newly arrived Gordons billeted on civilians. The Army took over the swimming baths, and the Liberal Club Room facilities were opened to the troops. The county was immediately divided into Military Districts: Perth City; Perth Area; Inchture (Lowland); and Aberfeldy (Highland), while horses, horse collars, furniture vans, motor cars, pit props, blankets, field glasses, bloodhounds and Perth's only motor boat were commandeered.

One other section of the community was quick off the mark: the grocery trade. The food scare in the city at the start of the South African War had not been forgotten, and, as in so many other areas, a near-panic was generated by price rises and the wealthy buying as much food as their wallets could afford and their larders hold. It did not take long for prices to soar, some by 100%, a pound of sugar rising from 2d to 4d. Merchants said that they would ration supplies to 7lbs (2s 4d) except for account-holders for whom a maximum of two cwt (£3 14s 8d) would be permitted. John Clark, manager of the Perth Co-operative Society, shamefacedly confessed that he had no option but to do likewise. However, he promised that he would consult his fellow-directors and would try to set a ceiling for the cost of basic foodstuffs such as oatmeal, flour and bread. Within hours, the price of a stone of flour or oatmeal rose by 6d to 2s 6d, bread by ½d for a 4 lb loaf, mutton by 1d per lb, ham by 2d, and eggs by 2d a dozen to 1s 6d. Ironically, this produced an even greater rush to hoard, and sugar could not be obtained in Perth for under 5d per lb, nor butter for less than 1s 8d. Worst of all was petrol, the price of two gallons rocketing overnight from 3s 4d to 10s. Perth Trades' Council at once protested and demanded that maximum prices be published and a citizens' committee formed to guard against exploitation. Their concern was justified. Drugs, bandages, coal, house rents and clothing had all risen by 25%. In some parts of the city, bread was actually 7d and there was widespread distress in working-class areas. Some unscrupulous traders were even watering milk supplies to increase profits.

Fortunately, the food panic subsided as quickly as it had flared. In no small measure this was due to the newspapers which lashed the selfish desire of wealthy people for storing huge supplies of provisions. The Government too played its part. Horrified by the scandal of national greed, it declared official price-levels: granulated sugar 4½d per lb, lump sugar 5d, butter 1s 6d, colonial cheese 9½d, bacon 1s 3d and margarine 10d. A storm of protest reached the Board of Trade. Sugar, in theory, might cost 35s per cwt but the real cost in Perth was 50s. This spurred the Co-operative to announce that henceforth, their sugar would sell at 4d per lb and their loaf at 6½d. Perhaps as a gesture of contrition, Lipton's, the city's largest grocery, offered to pay its employees half wages if they volunteered for the war. By 18 August, Canadian food supplies had arrived and before long, bread was cheap once again.

So far, to average citizens, the war had meant little more than a series of cancellations including the Perth Races, the Scone Flower Show, Perth Highland Games, Hunt Balls local football and rugby cup-ties. They were almost certainly unaware of the highly sophisticated propaganda machine operated by the nation's most creative minds, already at work exaggerating victories and minimising defeats. Neither would they appreciate the significance of recently hurried legislation, the Defence of the Realm Act (DORA), nor the fact that the railways were now under the Board of Trade and that all civilian contracts had been cancelled. Unless they were in business they were unlikely to know that there were restrictions on exports to the extent that any article could be seized and withheld from the market. They no doubt guessed that trading with the enemy was illegal, but would they have known that profiteering was too? Indeed, how many would have even understood this concept? Hardly anybody comprehended the financial labyrinth of the War Loan Act, the Currency and Bank Notes (Amendment) Act, the Finance (Session 2) Act and Loan Issues which authorised the State to borrow, almost without limit, cancel the Gold Standard, double income-tax and super tax, raise duties on beer and tea as well as placing the nation in debt for decades to come.

More mundane matters concerned the citizens. Allotments had to be made more productive and a campaign, 'Make Use of Your Garden' was launched. Scrap iron had to be collected systematically, health panels reorganised as young doctors and chemists left for the services, appeals devised to encourage thrift, cookery advice columns written for the newspapers and warning issued on the possibility of air attacks. Preparations also had to be made for military and civilian casualties. An ambulance train was prepared, the Old Northern District School was turned into a National Aid Society Hospital, the Sheriff Court became a temporary hospital, comfort parcels for the sick and wounded were collected and stored, Red Cross concerts were given in the City Hall to raise funds, the Old Infirmary became a Red Cross hospital and special beds were set aside for enteric fever victims. The city was ready.

The Black Watch were the first to leave for France following days of 'free fags, free suppers and free smokers' according to the *Perthshire Advertiser*. Crowds watched the departure of the 6th Black Watch. The 1st Black Watch (Reserves) left to the strains of 'Highland Laddie' and the thousand strong 2nd Black Watch (Reserves) to shouts of 'Smash the Germans' and showers of white heather. By 19 August, they were in France. Meanwhile, The Army Service Corps had problems. Seriously under-manned, they had to appeal for motor drivers and store men. By early November, they too had gone. The greatest effort, however, went into the formation of a new Mounted Highland Brigade of Scottish Horse, a task given to the Marquess of Tullibardine DSO, MP. Like many other units they lacked equipment and trained personnel and had no option but to scour the county in search of saddles and experienced blacksmiths under the age of fifty. By late October, even they were off. Strangely, the most detailed information on troop movements appeared almost daily in the press: 'Sixty troop trains pass through Perth every day,' 'The Camerons are coming,' 'The Highland Division is to be based at Bedford,' 'The Canadians have arrived in Perth,' 'Dundee is to be a submarine base,' 'Two thousand Seaforths pass through Perth from Fort George,' and 'Another five thousand troops are to be based here.' Before long, Perth was known as the 'Aldershot of the North.'

Newspapers were irresponsible in some respects. Clearly they had an obligation to keep up morale, stimulate patriotism, denigrate the enemy, justify the war and encourage recruiting, but they published every rumour that they heard, and some they even created, as if they were gospel truth. Thus, every week, they glowingly described some far-off, nameless, imaginary naval victory. They shamelessly exploited stories about the 'Russian Steamroller' of eight million men who were not only reported fighting in France, Belgium, East Prussia and Galicia, but were actually in the suburbs of Berlin. They painted dramatic pictures of life in Germany and a people demoralised, typhoid-stricken, suffering unemployment and starvation, and led by a Kaiser who was terminally ill. Their most ridiculous line of argument was that the powerful German Army was composed of cowardly officers who abused white flags, raped women, mutilated children and were cruel to prisoners. Any genuine report from France that praised the enemy's courage, ingenuity and kindness had little chance of publication.

The consequence of such reporting was the conviction that Scotland would soon be invaded by a rapacious foe. After all, enemy warships had been seen off the Tay and a U-boat had been sunk in the Forth. Some in Fife were already positive that there had been a landing at Largo Bay. As for Perth, everybody knew that it was the next target. Because of this, crowds flocked to see the film *If Britain Were Invaded* in the BB Cinema, and avidly read articles by 'experts' on 'How an Invasion Would Develop' and 'What Invasion Means.' Soon, Crieff, Blairgowrie and Perth all had Town Guards. Perth's Citizen Organisation for men over thirty, led by Dean of Guild Brown, made little progress because of lack of volunteers. Those who did volunteer were usually nearer seventy and were derisively called 'The OAPs' or 'The Balhousie Militia' because they trained in the grounds of Balhousie Castle, firing at cartoon figures of the Kaiser and the Crown Prince. Another fear encouraged by the press was 'The New Warfare' - attacks from the air. Bombing raids on London and Paris were reported in gruesome detail and consequently 'Monster Zeppelins' were reported as flying over Perth virtually every night. The image of death from the skies more than anything else persuaded the public that the Kaiser was a war criminal who should be deported to St Helena after the war.

One topic, so beloved by the press, degenerated into open hysteria. As with other communities, the hunt for spies took a real grip on Perth. Alarmist articles and editorials soon convinced the citizens that there really was a 'spy danger' and that spies were everywhere. Of particular concern was the threat of sabotage to the city's water supplies. To meet this possibility, the Town Council called out its thirty High Constables, armed with batons, to guard the reservoirs of Viewlands, Burghmuir and Muirhall. Because they had not seen active service against arsonists since 13 May 1852, and being considered costly and useless, they came in for a good deal of ridicule. A sharp editorial rebuke from the *Perth Courier* soon put an end to this with the claim that 'it cannot be said that this duty is either superfluous or without danger'. By mid-November, the High Constables had to have telephones and stoves installed and were paid 5s a day.

National hysteria was fuelled by prominent men like Lord Charles Beresford who claimed that there were thousands of German spies in the United Kingdom. This was a sentiment echoed by Perth's Norie-Miller who believed that British aristocrats could be spies as so many of them were German-related. No wonder wild stories abounded. Who fired on the steamer 'La Belle' from Dundee Esplanade? Who fired shots at a sentry in Meigle? Who was the suspicious character in Perth asking about the Royal Navy? Who tried to wreck a train on the Tay Bridge? Then the film *OHMS* in the BB Cinema simply made things worse. Mistakes were bound to happen: the American student arrested in Tay Street for asking where Scone Palace was on the map; the Englishman with a Kaiser moustache detained by the police; the Perth man apprehended in Montrose while on holiday; the drunk on the train who pulled the communication cord 'because he had seen spies'; and the besotted Army Service Corps recruit off to Bedford who attacked his fellow-passengers whom he suspected of spying. Sometimes suspicion was justified: the eighteen year old Robert Blackburn of Liverpool sold a plan of the Mersey Docks to the German Embassy; Lody, a spy, was shot in the Tower of London; Ernst, the Islington barber was given seven years at the Old Bailey for spying; and Nicholas Ahler, another spy, was sentenced to death. This last case convinced many people that there really were spies in their vicinity: Ahler had once lived in Methven. The national view was summed up by the *Daily Mail* on 16 October: 'The German spy network is so wide, so extraordinarily efficient, so immensely dangerous, that it cannot be too severely repressed.'

The excitement intensified with the arrival of the Belgians. At first most people repeated the words of Asquith, 'Brave Belgium', and looked forward to seeing the victims of German *Schrecklichkeit*. They eagerly read books about their guests' history, attended talks on their culture, tried Walloon recipes and donated money to the Belgian Relief Fund. It was a great disappointment when the first to appear, greeted at the railway station by the Earl of Mansfield and French-speaking Lady Georgina Drummond, were dispersed to Muthill, Pitlochry, Monzie and Dunblane. In fact, the first to come to Perth itself were Belgian soldiers, some shell-shocked and some maimed, who were lodged in the Old Infirmary in York Place. Before the year ended, no fewer than 172 had been treated there and their plight earned them a wide range of gifts and 'cinematograph treats' from the citizens.

The sudden arrival of some forty Belgian civilian refugees, including children, in mid-October, aroused an enthusiastic reception. Although their names were hard to pronounce: Skigipek; Leernputten; Terweduere; Delarq and Verlagen, their tales of fiendish German atrocities thrilled their listeners. There were stories of butchered children at Salins and cruel mass-rapes at Malines, not to mention descriptions of their homeland 'infested with spies'. Overcome with pity, the people of Perth laid on special treats for them, while local girls knitted comforts and the Town Council organised flag-days and concerts. Their numbers grew and by mid-November there were seventy-six, all supported by the Town Council. With interpreters in short supply, Canon Welsh and

Father Cotter took the lead in finding accommodation in St Johnston House, Rose Terrace, St Mary's Monastery, Kinnoull, Stormont Street Convent and St John's Restaurant, St John's Street. A few were even placed in splendid mansions, Monsieur Evrand at Rio, Monsieur Vaern at Keir and Monsieur de Coster at Cleeves. The arrival of a further thirty-seven refugees and their billeting in yet more fine villas, Inveravon and The Beeches, was too much for some. They were already weary of 'German rape and murder' recitations, which all too often, bordered on the absurd, as when a Liège woman claimed to have routed two thousand Uhlans with nothing more than a pot of hot water. There was talk in the city of the Belgians 'expecting to get a big house, rent free and fit for a king merely by asking.' Soon, partly because many of them had been given jobs at Friarton Glass Works, there were demands that no more be accepted. The situation was no different at Crieff where there were sixty-three Belgians.

Parallel to the fear of spies was the attitude to aliens in general. When the war started, the people of Perth had little real animosity for the Germans. For instance, there were no demonstrations of racial hatred when the first prisoners of war, nineteen trawler-men sent from Inverness, shuffled in chains from the railway station to vans bound for Perth Penitentiary. There was even sympathy for them. Again, when reports came to the city of the physical assaults on Germans and Austrians by mobs in London and Newcastle, many expressed disgust. However, the stories spread by the Belgians and the experiences of local people trapped on the Continent changed their attitude. Francis E Drummond-Hay of Seggieden, Consul in Stettin, reported that he had been detained by menacing crowds in Stettin while Mr and Mrs E A Zimmerman of Cornhill Terrace had been arrested in Berlin and robbed in Hamburg. Although the Police Register of Aliens shows that there were only ten Germans and one Austrian in Perth at that time, it was editorials against 'German crime and mendacity' and reports of dum-dum bullets and ravaged libraries that really sowed the seeds of hatred.

By now, some regarded all aliens as malevolent and many had their windows broken. Despite the fact that the majority of the public still regarded them as rather inoffensive, the foreigners were now too scared to venture far from home. Because some were convinced that

Austrian troops had used women and children as shields at the Battle of Dvina, there was an instant wave of fear when it was reported that a certain Joseph Capek, an Austrian waiter at the Palace Hotel, Pitlochry, had been found with a gun. Even the fact that it was only a licensed hunting-rifle did not save him from being charged with a breach of Section 23, Alien Registration Order (1914). Ironically, his ability to pay the £25 fine on the spot made many think that this was certain proof of his guilt. The State now exercised its powers through the Aliens Restrictions Act and the British Nationality and Status of Aliens Act. The former restricted the movements of aliens, while the latter limited the type of property they could own. Arrests were now common and Perthshire was 'swept' in late September. Seven were arrested in Callander, St Fillans, Pitlochry (an hotelier and son), Crieff (a lecturer) and six more in Dundee. All were taken to Perth Penitentiary. In Perth itself there were six other arrests: five Germans and an Austrian. These were two bottle-workers, a waiter, chef, barber and baker. They were all sent to Redford Barracks, Edinburgh, for interrogation.

Here again, many mistakes were made, such as the arrest of Edward Wolfsohn, who, despite his name, was an American citizen. Nevertheless, he was fined £81. Occasionally, there was a flash of compassion as when four elderly Germans from Portobello, 'a protected area', were permitted to earn their living in Perth as bottle-workers. Usually, there was just unnecessary harassment, as when dental surgeon Liebow and music professor Helman had their places of work occupied by troops. Such incidents eventually came to the attention of the German authorities and a formal protest was lodged. Of course, not all aliens were pliable and docile. On the Isle of Man, at the Aliens' Camp, some 4,000 inmates rioted at a cost of five dead and twelve injured. Some of the anti-German sentiments were downright silly, those of the musicians who smashed German pianos and the clerics who denounced the Kaiser as 'The Anti-Christ' for example. Despite all this, a fair number of Perth people seem to have kept their sense of humour, rather like the letter-writer in the *Perth Courier* on 25 August: 'I suppose that Frau Gretchen Schlosherkratz (a famous Berlin soprano) will be forbidden to appear on a British platform unless she wears a MacGregor tartan frock and alters her name to Mrs Maggie MacSporran.' But distrust extended far beyond the Germans. There were two stranded Russian timber-schooners in Perth harbour in destitute circumstances and their crews, continually drunk, turned to thieving and ended up in prison. So much for allies, thought the good folk of Perth.

There was one aspect of life which reacted quickly to the impact of war, and that was fashion. For men, formal dress - top hat and frock coat - disappeared almost overnight. For women, the change was slower, but equally dramatic. Clinging garments, theatrical hats and turbans, masses of hair, lethal hairpins, hobble-skirts and high-necked collars gave way to simpler, cheaper and more practical styles, even khaki shirts and tricolour ties. Patriotism became the in-word for society. There were patriotic evenings in the City Hall and Union Jack Days in the suburbs. Sunday sermons were usually on 'The Nature of Patriotism' or 'Military Service as a Duty'. Newspapers, when they were not expounding how glorious and heroic war could be, sold war maps for 1s and gave day-to-day reports on the situation. The commercial side of patriotism was also in evidence. Cairncross' jewellers advertised 'patriotic brooches', while McEwen's fashion store appealed to the public 'to buy dresses so that we can keep full employment of staff'. Most small businesses simply labelled their products 'British Made' and hoped for the best. Libraries recommended books like *With French at the Front* or *Mastery of the Air,* while enthusiastic, amateur poets churned out reams of rubbish such as *Wipe them out!* by David Sinclair and *Onward, Gallant Black Watch!* by James Carson.

The clergy found it hardest to adapt despite a stream of prayers for peace. A few volunteered for service at the Front, but for the rest, astonishingly, old animosities lingered and Roman Catholic priests refused to join their Protestant colleagues in a Christian Service. Some harangued their flocks on 'The Approach to Armageddon', others, such as the clergyman quoted in the *Perth Courier*, let fantasy go to their heads: 'The effect of the war will be a temperate society and one of industrial peace: everything could become perfect and new!' There were even some who seemed to regress to medievalism and saw something sinister in the chimes of St John's Kirk not running smoothly or found comfort in a 1657 prediction that proved the Kaiser was undoubtedly the devil. As one would expect, large numbers found a better hope in astrology.

Of the serious social problems affecting Perth in late 1914, the greatest involved drink. The Army had anticipated this. At the start of the war Colonel Hamilton had asked Perth Licensing Court to order the closure of pubs. They agreed to do so, but only from 6 p.m on Wednesday, 5 August, until 10 a.m on Friday, 7 August. When that day arrived, an even more senior officer, Colonel MacIntosh, CO No 1 District, made a second request. This time the Court agreed to close the pubs at 1 p.m on Saturday, 8 August. Still not satisfied, the Army then sent Major-General C J Mackenzie CB, CO Highland Division, to seek a two-week closure at 8 p.m. By now the Court resented the Army interference and simply granted one week's closure. Suddenly, the Army's worst fears erupted: the Police Court was flooded with cases of drunken excesses by troops. The Army persisted with their policy even though it caused discontent among some units. On Friday, 14 August, Captain Lyle, Assistant Provost Marshal, demanded pub closures at 5 p.m so that soldiers could clear the city. Although this request was backed by the Chief Constable, the Court would only accept 6 p.m on condition that public houses were not declared out of bounds to soldiers. They also promised to reconsider the matter every week. Sadly, the situation did not improve. The police disclosed the disturbing news that now the traditional, drunken, female vagrant was joined regularly by respectable female weavers. The military then confessed that all too often troops were too drunk to march, that they were continually attacking the police and were even breaking out of barracks in search of drink. Hordes of girls were said to have descended on the two Inches to taunt the troops as they trained, and requests went out for 'Women Patrols'.

Many were now convinced that it was time to follow the example of Russia and to ban drink for the duration of the war. Large meetings throughout the city demanded prohibition. Statistics appeared: 20% of the new patients at Murray Royal Asylum had drink-related illnesses; the cost for the nation annually was 32,000 lives; £165 million was spent every year on alcohol, £10,000 of which was spent weekly in Dundee alone. By 8 October, the Intoxicating Liquor (Temporary

Restrictions) Act was in force. This spurred the Temperance Association to demand a cut in drink sales on the grounds of evidence provided by the Association for the Protection of Women and Children that the streets of Perth were unsafe at night. Thus, they argued that pubs should all close at 8 p.m. The Licensing Court refused with local magistrates to blame. If a drunken thug, charged with wrecking a bar and assaulting customers, turned up in his regimentals, he was usually discharged. Little wonder such cases brought a reprimand from the Under-Secretary of State. This encouraged the Perth and District Association for the Protection of Women and Children to join with the ladies and workers of the Perth churches to stress again the conditions on the streets of Perth at night and the fears for the young women of the town. They told of publicans who allowed 'back-door drinking' after 10 p.m and the many sad stories of dirty and verminous children left alone by drunken mothers wasting allowance money sent to them by their husbands in France.

The drink trade was furious. They counter charged that early closing was bad for morale. But the problem would not go away and actually became worse with the arrival of each troop-train carrying soldiers on leave. There was nothing for it but to launch a temperance crusade in the city with a petition to the Government from the churches of Perth that excessive drinking was 'not only unpatriotic, but was helping the enemy.' That did it. Within hours, a glass of beer in Perth rose by ½d to 2d, a schooner by 1d to 3d, a bottle of beer from 1d to 4d, and an imperial pint of beer or stout to 4d. Sensing victory, the Rev W Lee and the Rev J Adie demanded 'Prohibition Now!' while Norie-Miller, through the press, warned that 'loose, drunken tongues help spies.' Although the publicans moaned that the whisky trade was depressed, the Chief Constable and Sheriff Johnston agreed to act and closed the pubs at 9 p.m. They went even further. Magistrates now warned that licences would be cancelled if any drunks were found on licensed premises.

Another social problem was poverty. The August food panic had produced disturbing headlines in the *Perth Courier*: 'Perth Feels the Pinch of War. Will Distress Become Acute?' Clearly, the families of serving soldiers were most at risk and the Town Council feared that many were already begging. With only 12s 6d weekly for a wife and 2s 6d per child, hardships involving food and rent were inevitable, so much so, that the Trades' Council, fully aware of the temptation to buy drink, suggested that food tokens replace money. On 10 November, the *Perth Courier*, in the face of the rapidly increasing number of widows and orphans, asked, 'Is the Poorhouse adequate provision?' An agitated Town Council unanimously agreed to petition the Government for at least 20s a week to dependants of men killed in the Forces. Although Separation Allowances were soon available under Circular No V, 1914, heartless landlords refused to ease the problem and Perth School Board was forced to open a Feeding Centre for Children at 106 South Street. Fortunately, the Prince of Wales' National Relief Fund was active in Perth, having received £1,000 from Sir John A Dewar and another £1,000 from the General Accident Insurance Company. In fact, by early September the Fund had almost £2 million at its disposal.

Amidst all this social turmoil great stress was laid on 'normality'. The Town Council, after announcing a policy of full pay for employees who were 'called up', strove to abide by it. With a huge drop in revenue and the absence of twenty-three key men, not to mention councillors, this was not easy. Still, they debated the purchase of a new fire-engine, two new dustcarts, a replacement for the city's refuse destructor, better lighting for the streets and more telephone boxes. They even discussed contingency plans for the post-war period. Some things, of course, never changed. Vandals still smashed telephone insulators, motorists still *scorched*, female vagrants still drank in the streets and poachers were still out after dark. Industrial unrest continued, although it was muted, among horse-shoers and painters and there was the occasional threat of a strike from the police.

Amusements and entertainment, so essential for morale, changed little except for the huge numbers of men in uniform. Mr Saville at Perth Theatre delighted his audiences with *Her Dreadful Secret, Charlie's Aunt* and *Captain Drew on Leave*, while Clara Butt attracted immense crowds to her evening concerts. The cinemas, so short of visual material from the Front, fell back on a sequence of biblical epics such as *The Photo Drama of Creation*, historical themes such as *The Battle of Shiloh,* or patriotic topics like *The Voice of Empire*. It was only in November that contemporary films, *To Arms!* and *Lord Kitchener's New Army* became available. People of all classes now queued to enjoy the visual stimulation, a factor not lost on local entrepreneurs who clamoured for licences to build new picture houses. In poor contrast were the traditional lantern exhibitions laid on by Kodak Supply Stores.

As for business and trade, house-building came to an abrupt stop through shortage of men and materials, and although some sectors panicked, the banks were not in too great a demand. Only the General Accident Insurance Company suffered when its Antwerp offices were looted by the enemy. At home, the fluctuating bank rate puzzled and concerned the business community as it made it difficult to peg the pound sterling to the US dollar. Despite the slogan 'business as usual', there was an element of industrial paralysis especially at the harbour. Some local hotels closed down, and because of scarcity of sugar, Campbells' Confectionary Works threatened to do the same.

The loss of skilled men was the most serious factor. The General Accident Insurance Company lost fifty-five, Lumsden of Huntingtowerfield (linen) lost twenty-eight, and Dewar and Sons (whisky) lost twenty-three. As for the latter, John Dewar himself went off to the Scottish Horse after promising that the jobs of volunteers would be held, and in the case of married men, their families protected. Moncrieff's North British Glass Works admitted that they were reasonably confident about their prospects, as were the dyers, Garvie and Deas. The two firms, however, had the benefit of confirmed government contracts. Shields' Wallace Works, on the other hand, was filled with gloom. It relied on foreign markets and it had no large stocks in store. Again, thirty of its best weavers were gone. At first it closed for a day or two, but after consultation with colleagues in Dunfermline, the management re-opened with a three-day week. Soon this became four days. Desperately short of flax and with many looms idle, Shields allowed his spinners to package Red Cross bundles. Coates' Balhousie Works shut down their twine and carpet manufacture departments and put the rest of the Works on short time. With the departure of fifteen of their men they petitioned the Government to suspend the Patents Act and cancel all German rights. This was a plea joined by Thomson's Fair City

Dyeworks, whose workers were also on short time. Deeply worried about possible rail dislocation, the management nevertheless encouraged staff to collect clothing for the Belgian refugees. The potential collapse of normal rail links was also the main concern of P and P Campbell, Dyers and Cleaners, whose employees were still on full time. With markets solely in the UK, they gloomily forecast 'a lot of mourning work' despite the shortage of dyes. By November, a quarter of their workforce had left for the forces and their girls were knitting flannel bed-shirts and jackets for the wounded.

But it was the effect of the war on Perth's largest firm that really worried the community. Trade had been dull at John Pullar and Sons, Dyers and Cleaners, in the earlier part of the year, but R D Pullar, chairman, had predicted that future prospects were bright. They too had a home-market. However, on the first day of the war, one hundred of their brightest and best, Reservists and Territorials, had gone off to fight. R D Pullar, perhaps in order to counter snide remarks about his family's German links, said he was glad to see them go. He then donated the firm's three large motor vans to the military and gifted the Parcel Post store in Carpenter Street to the Red Cross. Even the Workers' Rest Room was turned into the Black Watch Club and Recreation Room where soldiers could enjoy hot meals, gramophone and piano music. Furthermore, he bought 2,500 cuts of wool for his girls to knit comforts: 1,326 pairs of socks; 325 helmets and 85 belts - 1,736 bundles in all. With each went a gift of soap from the firm, cigarettes and white heather, together with names and addresses of the girls.

Before long, the feared dislocation of rail traffic took place and Pullars had to go on short time. R D Pullar was not downcast; he had ample stocks of dyes and before long big government orders were bound to lead to a boom in dyeing. However, he was losing men at an alarming rate. By 24 August, no fewer than 118 had left. Of these, fifty-seven went to the 6th Black Watch, twenty-four to the Army Service Corps, twenty-three to the Scottish Horse, five to the Army Reserve, three to the Highland Cyclist Corps, two to the Royal Army Medical Corps and one each to Transport, Yeomanry, Naval Reserve and Royal Scots. By 26 August, the number had risen to 130 and by 14 November it was 170. As in other firms, senior staff went too: H S Pullar to the Scottish Horse,

G D Pullar to the 6th Black Watch and J L Pullar to the 4th Black Watch. The entire Pullar family did their bit: A E Pullar helped at recruiting rallies and gathered money for the ambulances, *The Fair Maid of Perth* and *Hal o' the Wynd*. R M Pullar devoted himself to the welfare of the Belgian refugees. The Pullar womenfolk visited the wounded and organised concerts. Thanks to massive coal stocks at Tulloch, dry-cleaning coped well, but as early as 7 October, it was obvious that a dye famine was near. Two weeks later it hit Perth and dyes thereafter were in short supply. R D strongly supported the theme of 'business as usual' but argued that after the war Britain should make its own dyes to beat the German monopoly. It was the start of many trips south to the Board of Trade in an attempt to set up a joint stock company for aniline dyes.

Although casualty figures from Mons were released near the end of August, details were not known for another month. Tragically, some of the dead, maimed or missing men had only been weeks in uniform. Others had married hours before departure. Soon, severely wounded men were hospitalised at Coupar Angus, Aberdeen and Ochtertyre House, by Crieff. Many of these men were to die from their wounds, but it was the horrifying number listed as 'missing' that caused most upset. Death did not discriminate as to class. The Master of Kinnaird, a captain in the Scots Guards and Major Lord Charles Mercer were listed as 'killed in action' along with a Forgandenny postman and a Crieff shepherd. Inevitably, it was the 6th Black Watch that most concerned the people of Perth. They knew that they had had their baptism of fire at Mons and they had read in the *Perth Courier* that they had been 'cheery amid flying shell ... terrifying the Germans with the bayonet' and 'leading a stirrup charge at Mons.' They were proud of the decorations the men had won and marvelled at their endurance in the Flemish winter. However, none could ignore the truth: many of the Reservists, including their Commanding Officer, Lieutenant Colonel A Grant Duff, were now dead.

The Army began the process of raising 100,000 volunteers as early as 25 August. Three days later, they asked for another 100,000. By the end of September, 500,000 had volunteered and by the end of the year, the number had risen to 1,186,000. Perth played its part. Festooned with posters and banners, the city began to build its own 'citizen army'.

Almost every member of the County Cricket Club together with dozens of junior footballers came forward. The local gentry: His Grace, the Duke of Atholl, Lord Lieutenant of Perthshire; Lady Tullibardine; Lady Dewar and many others offered their services in the form of personal appeals. Nevertheless, it was the unexpected news of the retreat from Mons in early September that brought the realisation that a mighty effort would be needed to end the war as promised by Christmas, and the press responded with a passionate 'Call to Arms!' Every week, recruiting parties similar to 18th century press-gangs, combed the countryside describing the rosy life of the soldier and urging enlistment before the war ended. In the City Hall there were scenes of wild enthusiasm and emotion at rallies as men actually struggled with each other to take the King's Shilling in what the press called 'another great demonstration and recruiting drive'. In one week, as many as 672 recruits presented themselves at the Barracks: thirty-five of them had come from Wales. Some families, the Wiltshires, McCabes and Sinclairs, sent four sons apiece. Men poured in from Abernethy, Balbeggie, and Methven and in less than six weeks 64,444 had enlisted in Scotland. By late September, no part of the county could escape a full-scale recruiting drive.

The first, well-organised recruiting drive in Perth, complete with parades, banners and famous orators, was held on the North Inch on 26 October. In the heady excitement, sixty men offered themselves to the colours and were proud to see their names printed in the press. In November, every household in the city received a recruiting circular announcing that the Army would now take 'bantams' of five feet three inches. This brought a further 136 Perth men into the net. Local churches, caught up in the fever, actually placed advertisements in the newspapers boasting of the number of their congregations who had 'gone off to war.' For the United Free Church alone there were sixty-six from St Paul's, fifty-seven from the West Church, and fifty-three from the North Church. Rural Perthshire rushed to compete, with one man enlisting from Forgandenny United Free Church, two from Kinclaven and three from Logiealmond. Furthermore, parishes vied with each other to rush men into uniform. Blair Atholl sent sixty-one, Balquidder, thirty-two and Collace, ten. Even schools were not immune and by late December, 211 former pupils from Perth Academy were off. By

Christmas, some rural areas were almost denuded of young men. Bankfoot had given seventy-eight men, Braco, forty-one and even remote Rannoch, thirty-five. But not all were patriotic. As early as November, 'Random Notes', the foreign affairs column, was deploring the fact that 'Perth possesses quite a number of able-bodied shirkers.'

Recruiting Rally, Perth

This infuriated some middle-class ladies and in packs they searched high and low for 'dodgers'. The issue divided the community, but most thought that giving white feathers to young men was an insane idea of hysterical females. Even the authorities were alarmed and issued a statement deploring these unofficial recruiting methods. They preferred men inspired by patriotism or a desire for excitement. They would even accept men desperate to escape boring jobs or those pressured by their employers to enlist. Some volunteers found it hard to forget their thieving habits while in uniform, but all too often their fines were paid for them by patriots or else they were simply admonished. Others found that their courage failed them at the sight of a vaccination needle and they were sent home. Of course, bogus heroes were common as they cadged free drinks or flirted with the girls. They, in sharp contrast, received little mercy from the courts. The same was true for deserters. D Block in Perth Penitentiary was reserved for military offenders and there were plenty of them. Not surprisingly, as early as November, some newspapers were asking if conscription should be introduced.

As the year drew to a close, the *Perth Courier* reviewed the previous five months. It tried to comfort the readers by claiming that things had not been as bad as had been anticipated: 'There had been no sustained increase in the cost of food, no run on the banks, no massive business failures, no higher unemployment, no air raids, no starvation, no looting and no rioting.' What it failed to list was the growing sense of realism in the city. There was a growing awareness of the dreary rubbish being published, the National Anthem being 'absurd and flat' and scepticism toward the belief that the war was creating a more democratic society. The fire had gone out of newspaper reports and the enemy were 'Germans' again rather than 'Huns' and the supposed letters from the Front no longer spoke of 'killing Germans like rats' or 'mowing down German hordes' or 'our troops more like mad Zulus than human beings.' There was no more about 'the German guns having as much effect on us as a daisy air rifle.' Clearly, the novelty of war was wearing off.

1915

The City was now a gigantic armed camp with thousands of soldiers milling around, some training for the Front, others recuperating from wounds and most enjoying their leave. All shared the conviction that their life expectancy was limited and they were determined to cram as much excitement as they could into their remaining days. Such an attitude created serious problems for both military and civil authorities. For the former, there was the loss of control over supposedly disciplined units; for the latter, there was the clear drop in moral standards.

The worst offenders were the Scottish Horse, described by the *Constitutional* on 6 January as 'a damned nuisance due to drink', a view which provoked the editor to predict that '1915 is going to be a drunken year.' When asked for an explanation for their outrageous behaviour, their Commanding Officer, Lord Tullibardine, condemned 'the city's lack of facilities and floods of undesirable women.' The Town Council were quick to refute this, stating that the charges were unwarranted and should be retracted. Tullibardine refused, and in a press interview asserted that 'Perth does nothing to keep my men from pubs and bad women.' This was too good a chance to miss and the *Perth Courier* editorial asked the key question: 'Are Women of Perth Immoral?' Naturally, the editorial denied this and urged that Tullibardine be charged with slander. At this stage some church leaders intervened to lower the temperature. They suggested that the root of the matter lay in the large numbers of bored troops in Perth and Scone. But the more outspoken United Free Church Presbytery would have none of it. They thought that the Scottish Horse deserved condemnation. Police investigations showed otherwise.

Far too many publicans were refusing to close their premises as they should at 9 p.m and were encouraging late-night drinking. Their motive was obvious: they had never made so much money before. By February, the position had worsened. A campaign was launched by the organisers of the 'National Patriotic Pledge against Drink' with the slogan: 'Drink too much – get drunk – help the enemy!' Neither this nor massive demonstrations had any effect. Indeed, further police reports suggested that there was a surge in bigamous marriages in the Perth area which the culprits, when charged, put down to excessive drink.

The self-elected guardians of public morality now entered the scene. After excited meetings in various church halls, groups of 'respectable, middle-class church ladies' decided to form a 'moral watch' and to patrol the streets at night. This proved to be a dangerous undertaking. The streets were full of noisy, unkempt soldiers reeling from drink as they pursued tipsy mill girls and hard-faced harlots drawn to the city by easy money. Eye-witness reports by these ladies made embarrassing reading for the Army, and worried by the adverse publicity, the Provost Marshall ordered the Military Police to clear all the pubs of troops by 7 p.m. Again, the editor of the *Perth Courier* asked a pertinent question: 'Why not put the pubs out of bounds? It's done elsewhere.' Teachers added a warning that there had been an enormous increase in juvenile smoking and pleaded that this too be banned. The police, however, confessed that with their current powers they simply could not stop 'back-door drinking'. They also disclosed that the railway refreshment room was being abused with drink. The news that many soldiers were so drunk that they missed their trains brought more calls for 'Prohibition in the City'. The threat of prohibition made the publicans strive harder to close by 10 p.m at least. One interesting statistic emerged – the city had never had so many applications for licences from would-be publicans and this simply made the job of the police more difficult. There was another dimension: gambling. Douce citizens were appalled to see crowds of soldiers playing pontoon and crown and anchor on the Inches, finishing up with fistfights. The fact that the worst offender in the city was the Barracks' canteen convinced many that it was 'now time to appeal to the Defence of the Realm Act.'

This did not please the Army at all and they were no doubt delighted when the news broke that the new King's Cinema would open on 12 May. Senior officers recommended the cinema, this 'innocent amusement' to their men and were convinced that the drink problem would disappear. Within days they realised that they were wrong. In fact, intemperance among soldiers was steadily increasing. A last effort to control the situation was made: price rises. The cost of a glass of whisky rose to 6d, and a bottle of Special Whisky from 2s 6d to 6s 6d. There was still no improvement, and by June it was realised that something really drastic was needed. Lloyd George was said to have considered buying out the drinks' industry because of its devastating effect on absenteeism, but found the prospect too costly. There was one alternative left: the establishment of a Central Control Board (Liquor Traffic).

By mid-June, The Defence of the Realm Act had closed all the city pubs by 7 p.m. Drink prices suddenly soared again. Whisky rose to 9d a gill, brandy to 8d a glass and gin to 5d a glass and to 4s a bottle. Licensing hours were also cut and the beer diluted. The YMCA, YWCA, Salvation Army and Church Army all celebrated. Drunkenness fell away as did the number of convictions in the courts. It was not until August that the issue flared again when it was discovered that the 'walking wounded' were getting drunk on the spirits bought for them by admiring civilians anxious to hear their tales of warfare. This was an area which seemed to be beyond the powers of The Central Control Board (Liquor Traffic), but in an attempt to limit the damage, pubs were officially told that they could only open on weekdays from 12 noon to 2.30 p.m and from 6 p.m to 9 p.m. As for weekends, they were restricted to 2 p.m to 7 p.m.

By October, there was even a 'No Treating Order' which meant that no civilian in a hotel, restaurant, pub or club was to be served a drink without purchasing a meal. The pressure on drinkers increased as the winter drew near. As in France, no spirits were to be sold in the city outwith the hours of 12 noon to 12.30 p.m and 6.30 p.m to 9.30 p.m from Monday to Friday. More duties were imposed, prices were raised further and beer diluted again. In the city, the extra 3d on a bottle of whisky brought squeals of protest from local publicans. They fought back with a clever tactic which damaged the relationship between the Army and the community. They argued that the regulations imposed by the Central Control Board (Liquor Traffic) were a breach of local byelaws. A clash seemed inevitable.

Gowrie Inn, Perth

There had been signs as early as February that the Town Council were getting tired of the never-ending demands of the military. For instance, the Commanding Officer of HQ Company, Highland Division Train, informed the Town Council that he wanted the Large City Hall immediately as a billet for the Army Service Corps. Rather annoyed, the Town Council responded with a demand that the Army pay 3d per man per night, pointing out that this venue was the biggest hall in the city and as such, the main source of civic income. The Army refused. The Town Council were then forced to accept 2d per man per night. Meanwhile, the public at large were not really concerned about the matter because of the build-up in troop movements. People were aware that the 4th Black Watch (Dundee) had been ordered to France to join with the 1st Black Watch and the 2nd Black Watch. Something was brewing and the Black

Watch were going to be heavily involved. March brought news of the bloody battle of Neuve Chapelle and the now customary long casualty lists in the newspapers.

The Army in Perth then decided not to pay the agreed rate for the Large City Hall and instead offered a lump sum of £5 10s 0d. The Town Council, realising that the military were spending vast sums daily in the city, agreed. Yet, two weeks later the Army Service Corps changed its mind and decided to go elsewhere. The Town Council pointed out that they could hardly control their expenditure unless they had a regular income and the Army accepted this. Although HQ Company of the Highland Division Train decided that they would accept the Large City Hall, after inspecting the premises they declared that it was too big for their needs and they requested the Lesser City Hall for which they offered only £2 10s 0d. When the Town Council protested at this constant change, the Army claimed that they had to cut costs. The focus of dispute then shifted abruptly to Charlotte Street. Here, Brigadier-General Stockwell, OC Highland Division, had an office from which he announced to the press that Perth was suitable as a centre for troop concentration. This statement puzzled the Town Council: what could it mean? After all, there were already large numbers of troops in the city. When approached for clarification, Stockwell said that 'the decision has been cancelled.'

Another flashpoint, almost comical given the backcloth of war, revolved around the right of members of the Army Pay Corps to be admitted into the local Baths for 2d. It sparked off a considerable amount of resentment for a few days until frenzied troop movements in the city made the public realise that another 'Big Push' was coming. There was talk of the transfer of the Crieff Territorial Army to Bedford to join up with the 51st Highland Division and the departure of the 5th Black Watch (Forfar), 6th Black Watch (Perth) and the 7th Black Watch (Fife) to join the 8th Black Watch and the 9th Black Watch. Where could they be going? The public soon knew - Festubert. Once again, there were pages listing the dead, the missing, the wounded or prisoners of war.

By June, the Town Council were complaining about the number of horses which the Army had picketed on the South Inch. The Army reply was that 'picket-in-open' was standard practice. A few weeks later the same topic came up in regard to the North Inch. A company of Royal Engineers were now billeted in the Northern District School and they picketed their mounts on the North Inch close to the river where they could practise pontoon and trestle building. The Town Council's concern over its dearest recreational areas and local salmon and whisky industries were ignored. There was also the problem that the Army had commandeered every horse in the region and none could be acquired at any price.

By August there was another surge in the numbers of wounded pouring into the city's crowded hospitals, forcing the Army to take over the city's Poorhouse and turn it into another military hospital. Then came September and the 'ghastly failure' at Loos. Black Watch casualties were enormous, indeed, they were so severe that the 4th Black Watch and the 5th Black Watch had to amalgamate survivors into the 4th/5thBlack Watch. Most households in the city mourned the loss of a relative or a friend and the Army's decision to transfer the Highland Fife Battery of the Royal Garrison Artillery to the City Hall hardly seemed important. Far more ominous was the transfer of the 2nd/6th Seaforths (Territorial Army), all 500 of them, to Crieff with 100 members of the Army Service Corps from Perth. It seemed likely that another 'great attack' was being planned, but where were the men to come from?

The Town Council, despite its occasional brush with the military, were determined to do what they could to help. After all, there was a fascinating new concept now in general use, 'manpower.' In mid-January they asked the Parliamentary Committee for a list of all men of military age and suggestions for eminent speakers who could come to Perth. They also sent a 'manifesto' to every householder explaining that the war was at a crisis and that more men must be found. To back this up, the Town Council released a flood of posters. These were everywhere: on trams, vans, buses, telegraph poles and house walls.

Recruiting schedules went out to family heads, war lectures were planned and more posters distributed. Some reckon that by the autumn, the country had fifty-four million on display. A string of skilled orators came to Perth, men like Sir Edward Parrot, Chairman of the Edinburgh United Liberal Association, soon to be an MP. Within days of his rousing address the Town Council had set in motion two more well-organised recruiting drives. Even the city's wards had their own local drives and the directors of the Caledonian Railway Company agreed to show posters in their trains and stations. Hard as it is to imagine, the city churches also joined in and were giving colourful calls to arms by early May. But it was not enough.

First World War Poster

The fiasco at the Dardanelles and the stalemate at Ypres were ample proof that the war machine, as ever, needed more and more men. The only agency that could provide them was the State, which turned to the idea of 'Mobilisation of National Resources' to find out exactly what the nation could afford. Thus, queries came to Perth from the Committee on War Organisation in the Distributing Trades of Scotland as to how many men of military age were employed in the city's shops. There was also a request that the Town Council encourage its most skilled workmen to volunteer for munitions' work. This they did, although they appreciated that success would merely add to their own problems. It was not to be: only two came forward, a water engineman and a gas worker. All over the country, it was the same. The fire had gone out of the nation's spirit. The war was no longer a noble crusade.

The Government knew that the war had taken a serious turn and that there was a sense of gloom in the land. In early July therefore it started the process of compiling the National Register of all persons, male and female, aged sixteen to sixty-five, with details of their occupations and whether they were willing to do work of national importance. Already it contained the seeds of its own failure with far too many potential exemptions, a fact which did not seem to dawn on the thousands of unpaid distributors and collectors of this massive enquiry. In Perth 'The Great Recruiting Drive' of late August had appeared to prove otherwise as young men, intoxicated by the patriotic tunes played by the visiting Scots Guards Band, still offered themselves for service. Older heads may have reflected differently at the Jeanfield Gala Day for the Troops when there were too many limbless men present, a painful reminder of the reality of the trenches. Stories of a local man, a dyer, called Imrie, who had six sons in uniform, and the oratory of former sheriff and now Lord of Appeal in Ordinary, Lord Dunedin of Stenton, no longer worked. Two million had volunteered: there would be no more. This irritated some and Lady Jellicoe especially raved against the 'Perth loafers.' The Town Council furiously rejected the charge. But everybody knew that cold reality had now settled over the nation.

Sophisticated methods using psychologically compelling posters such as 'Your Country Needs You!' and peer-group pressure of the Pals' Battalions were not enough. The next logical step was to check the

National Register and root out those not engaged in essential work. Each of these was then asked 'to attest', that is to affirm their willingness to accept military service when called. Clearly there was an element of compulsion or implied threat, but given the principle that married men would be the last to go, most men accepted the policy. The Director of Recruiting, Lord Derby, was therefore able to keep up his 'drives for volunteers.' On 19 October, the *Perth Courier* revealed that, under Lord Derby's 'New Civilian Recruiting Scheme', at least another 1,000 men were required from Perthshire immediately. Although some of the city's most prominent citizens, A E and R M Pullar, were members of the Local Recruiting Appeal Committee which acted as a Tribunal, few could be persuaded to come forward willingly. The first to do so, under the city's 'Derby Scheme', was the city's lamp trimmer. Despite the fact that others shared his fate - the swimming baths' superintendent and his assistant, the blacksmith, a machine fitter and the tramway manager - it was soon obvious that this scheme too was failing. The resignation of the Home Secretary, Sir John Sinclair, then confirmed the Town Council's suspicion that conscription was on its way.

'Business as usual' for the Town Council meant a continuation of the work they had been doing in 1914, that is, guarding the reservoirs, organising cycle parades for the Red Cross, supervising the School Children's War Guild, collecting scrap metal and encouraging the Thrift Campaign. Although they had magnificent support from most of the city's leading families, the Pullars for instance, nevertheless, the situation was very difficult. A E Pullar met the wounded when they arrived in Perth, while his wife dealt with their family problems. R D Pullar gave 'extras' to those in the Military Hospital and R M Pullar tried to help the Belgian refugees. The Council had to keep on top of masses of regulations, many with a strong rural quality such as the Parasitic Mange Order (1911), the Poisons and Pharmacy Act (1908) or the Fabrics (Misdescription) Act (1913) while worrying about the extension of underground telegraph lines or gas power to the outer suburbs or more seats on the North Inch or even planning new streets in the city. Problems dominated their lives. Where could they obtain more petroleum? Should they allow the inmates of Murray Royal Asylum to keep cows for milk? Should they organise a local Labour Force? How should they handle river pollution scares? Should they take out insurance against air raid damage? Where would they find extra staff to run the National Registration Scheme? Should they allow dogs on trams? Should they ask the Government to consider the Electric Department as part of munitions? Where could they get more coal?

Busy as they were, they had more immediate challenges to face. Their typists were increasingly unhappy with 35s a week. After all, in munitions, they would have earned 40s. Tram staff were also restless. They asked the Town Council for a rise 'to bring the men into line with other towns.' Some depot fitters and blacksmiths were demanding 2s and, in their discussions, the Town Council began to wonder if a 'war bonus' might not be the answer. Then the press suddenly disclosed that there was unrest on the railways following the National Union of Railwaymen's discovery that the cost of living in Perth gave the £ a value of 16s 3d. In fact, their real wage, they calculated, was barely 7s 9d weekly. This disclosure brought a flood of wage-demands: the grave-diggers offered to work Saturdays for an extra 7d; carters and scavengers each wanted a rise and soon it was the turn of the lamp trimmers. Before long, the Town Council felt that, given the cost of living, they had to take some kind of action. They therefore offered 2s more to roadmen whose pay was under 35s a week. Gossip in the city called this 'a war bonus', but that was officially denied. The 2s weekly rise awarded to the city's cowherds passed unnoticed. The same could not be said for the next demand - from the police. Short of men and bedevilled with masses of regulations such as the Police (Emergency Provisions) Act (1915) and the Special Constables (Scotland) Act (1915), they wanted their 33s 3d wage increased to 36s 9d. The situation was serious as the police were considering strike action if they were refused. The Town Council warned against such a step, but did concede that if any of them were called up, their military service would count towards the pension. For the moment, this satisfied them.

Dissatisfaction soon spread to the private sector. The bakers, anxious to copy what they thought were roadmen gains, demanded a war bonus of 4s on the 33s basic wage. The most radical workforce in the city, the printers, announced that they formally objected to the high cost of living and denounced as 'dilution' the introduction of female labour into their trade. Then, shortly after a mildly comical strike by newsboys, came word that one trade was to be given official war bonus payments. Messrs T P Miller and Company, Turkey Red Dyers, Cambuslang, Glasgow, informed the Amalgamated Society of Dyers that they would give 1d an hour to all dyers, 15% on piece rates, 10% bonus on wages under 35s weekly and 5% on wages above that figure. This war bonus was to be paid out every fourth Saturday. The Town Council were horrified and declared that 'No war bonus will be paid to any employee.' It was the signal for a massive wave of substantial wage demands compared to 1914 levels. Printers, for instance, wanted 4s 2d on a minimum wage of 32s 6d, a 12.8% increase. Employers were aghast and offered 1s 6d which was rejected. As the Town Council knew that they would have to react quickly, they asked their convenors to assess the situation to see who deserved pay rises. Nine from the Lighting Department were listed. Then, in September, came a really serious threat. The National Union of Gas and General Workers of Great Britain and Ireland threw down the gauntlet: they wanted a rise of 1d an hour for their members. The Town Council decided to bluff it out and announced that there would be no increase of wages during the war. At the same time they appealed to the Minister of Munitions for help although plumbers had already won another ½d an hour, taking them to 9½d an hour. At this point the focus of attention switched elsewhere when the printers, as a trade, denounced house rents in Perth.

House rents had become an issue, particularly in the west of Scotland, over the previous few months because rents had risen by 20% leading to many evictions and, consequently, violent protests. In Perth, landlords were not reputed to be war profiteers. They were, at worst, simply uncaring and negligent. The Town Council tried hard to keep up housing standards. They ordered the owners of eleven houses in Meal Vennel to make them fit for human habitation and condemned outright others in Thimblerow and Skinnergate. In April, they launched a campaign to install WCs in all the houses in Union Lane, Mill Street, North Port and Bridge Lane, the poorest parts of the city. By May they had factual proof that most of the city's TB patients came from desperately overcrowded homes, often lacking decent sanitation. Nationally, something had to be done. In November, the Government issued the Rent and Mortgage Interest (War Restrictions) Act. It meant that mortgages could not be foreclosed nor interest payments increased. Rents on Scottish houses under a Rateable Value of £30 per annum were also limited. The Act had several unseen results. Speculative building for the working classes continued until well into the 1930s and although there was better tenure, it also led to job mobility. In fact, rent control was not a great success. There was no penalty for contravening the Act which was regularly breached. Housing costs rose, there was more overcrowding and the reduced profit-level for landlords led to fewer repairs and, eventually, even greater disrepair. The repercussions for health were obvious. Local authorities did, however, set up depots for the sale of milk for infants at cost price. Even the decision that stillbirths had to be notified was generally approved.

Problems with health and housing were not helped by the insidious, constant rise in the cost of living throughout 1915 which hurt working-class families so much. Bread, for example, by January, was up 30% on the July 1914 price-level, not to mention wide variations even within the county. In Blackford 7½d was paid for a loaf, in Crieff and Methven, 8d, and 8½d in Northern Perthshire. Coal was worse as it was so scarce. Because of the scarcity, railwaymen received a war bonus of 2s in February by which time the price of coal was up 15%. Consequently, the city was short of gas as prices rose and production fell. In March, coke rose by 1s 8d a ton, matched by an increase in carting charges. By the autumn it was obvious that the colder weather would bring a coal shortage and the Government warned communities to prepare for the worst. That came, somewhat abruptly, in October: 'Fuel Famine - No Coal!'

Foodstuffs were bad too. In January the price of beef rose by 1d per lb and so alarmed were the City of Perth Co-operative Society that they wrote to several MPs demanding immediate action. The *Perth Courier* again took the lead: 'Bloodsucking Traders - The Bloated Beasts of Perth.' With flour up 75%, sugar 72% and meat 12%, their charge seemed justified. The Town Council and Perth Labour Council confirmed the profiteering, except for sugar, which they claimed had risen 200% in Perth. It was useless for realists to point out that price rises had a great deal to do with the U-boat campaign which had started in February or for the Government to remind the public that Germany had had bread-rationing since January. While, in retrospect, it is clear that Britain had no real scarcity, but just stiff price rises, it was enough for the State to launch a propaganda campaign for economy.

Skinnergate, from Mill Street end, 1924

Photograph courtesy of Perth Museum & Art Gallery, Perth & Kinross Council, Scotland

This brought little consolation despite news of food riots in Chemnitz and Berlin. Soon there was a petition to the Prime Minister requesting His Majesty's Government to exercise their powers and regulate the price of these commodities and thus prevent unnecessary hardships among householders.

Throughout March, the *Perth Courier* kept up its campaign especially against 'Grasping Bakers'. Every trade union in the city joined in, particularly the Scottish Typographical Union who wrote to the Prime Minister. But, there was no improvement. By June prices were up 32% over the year: butter rose 2½d, bacon 3d to 4d per lb, cheese 3d, pork sausages 2½d and cooked meat, 4d to 6d. Some calculated that food costs were actually rising at 1s 3d a week for most families. By July the price of food in a year had risen by 34%. Nationally, meat and bread were up 40%, fish 60%, flour 45% and sugar 68%. Clothing was no different. By September it was estimated that clothing was up 70% on the August 1914 level. For instance, a yard of blue serge, once 4s 3d, was now 8s 4d. One could purchase plenty of wool, but absolutely no dyes. Then, as with coal, October and the approach of winter brought a surge in the cost of food. A gallon of milk rose from 10d to 1s and eggs were now 3d each. The *Perth Courier* again got to the crux of the matter on the 16 November. How could a soldier's widow survive on 10s a week? How could she and four children live on 22s 6d a week? There were even worse scenarios. An orphan only received 5s weekly, a totally disabled soldier, 25s, a partially disabled soldier, 'a discretionary payment' of 3s 6d to 17s 6d. Society was suffering.

As one might expect, there was now considerable hatred for Germans. Much of it in Perth seemed to be due to a leaflet, 'Advice on Air Raids by Germans' which was distributed to every householder in the city. It painted a picture of unrelieved terror. The German language, now a mark of contempt, was no longer studied. Although some writers call this reaction 'wartime xenophobia', for aliens in Perth it meant a life of misery with many restrictions. However, their worst time came in May. The Germans were using poison gas at the Front, they had just sunk the *Lusitania* at a cost of 1,000 innocent lives and British losses in Flanders were extremely high. The combination of these factors was too much for some and German pork butchers in the South Street had their premises attacked by a mob. In July a local clairvoyant achieved fame when she predicted that the Kaiser would soon die and the war end. German had long since been dropped from the curriculum and local merchants refused to sell any goods that had their origin in Germany.

As for the Russians stranded at Perth harbour, the Town Council were completely disenchanted with them and decided that their previous ruling of 'no dues to be charged on the two ships' was cancelled. From henceforth, they would have to pay ½d per ton per month. Given the fact that they were penniless, nobody could explain how they could pay, and, frankly, nobody cared. Patience with the Belgians was also running out. Their wounded soldiers in the Old Infirmary were grateful enough, but there were no more visits to the Belgian Village Exhibition in Glasgow. The people of Perth were irritated by the fact that, despite the high cost of gas, the refugees in 2 Rose Terrace, Inveravon Bank, Bridgend, St Leonard's Bank, 4 High Street and 8 Watergate had been charged only at half the current rate. When they discovered that Lady Georgina Drummond had arranged that they only paid carriage prices for coke, they were furious. Before long Belgians were actually being assaulted in the streets.

Business and industry had to work on against this background of unrest while many senior staff were at the Front. Among them were: G Pullar, Captain 6th Black Watch; J L Pullar, Lieutenant, 4th Black Watch; R S Pullar, Major, 3rd Scottish Horse; A Shields, Lieutenant, Lowland Royal Garrison Artillery; and D Shields, Lieutenant, 15th Royal Scots. At the North British Dye Works (Pullars) the workers were upset by rumours of enormous profits being made by dyers. Absent, as he had to attend the Board of Trade in London, R D Pullar was unable to deny these allegations. He was, in fact, fighting furiously to defend the National Dye Scheme in which he believed. All he could do was to warn the city that there was 'an impending famine in dyes.' The national debate on how to organise the dye industry was fierce with discussions held at London, Leeds and Bradford. The *Perth Courier* grasped the seriousness of the situation in its headline: 'Perth and Dyeing Trade Crisis!' But, perhaps the Perthshire *Advertiser* was nearer the mark on 23 January: 'It is possible that the industrial effects of the war on Perth may prove greater than the military.' By February R D Pullar's work bore fruit when the National Dye Scheme was approved by the formation of a new company, British Dyes Ltd. In Perth, however, so short were they of true dyes, all kinds of substitutes were in use, herbs, mosses and trees.

The strain on the chairman, R D Pullar, must have been immense. A steady flow of casualties was reported among his 179 men at the Front and there was growing criticism in Parliament of his new dye company. Although the firm was busy, there were problems. Unfit men were being lured south by the prospect of a wide choice of jobs and higher wages, while apprentices simply refused to attend any kind of evening class, even those essential for their trade. Not that the workforce was in any way unpatriotic. One dyer had six sons in uniform and there were many letters of appreciation for gifts, such as from the crew of HMS *Triumph*, torpedoed at the Dardanelles, or the men of 1st/6th Black Watch.

July brought more headaches. The Munitions' Act had brought in a whole range of regulations for firms employed in war production. For a while, there was some confusion as to whether dyeing uniforms and cleaning blankets came under this category. But, apparently it did. The workforce was unhappy with the suggestion of compulsory arbitration of industrial disputes, the fact that it was now a penal offence to leave a job without the employer's permission and 'a leaving certificate', and the threat of dilution. July also brought a sharp reminder that profits were falling because there was now virtually no private dyeing. There were not even enough horses left in the city to pull the firm's fire-engine and R D Pullar had no option but to buy a motor tractor. With October came the coal crisis and production fell significantly. Sadly, it coincided with a wave of casualties, particularly from 8th Black Watch. No wonder the firm's end-of-year report contained the observation that '1915 has been the worst year in the history of the company.'

Conditions were much the same at P and P Campbell's Dye Works where the girls knitted for the troops. One director and forty men had left, some 25% of the total staff. Not that it mattered much when there was no demand for cleaning evening wear, and dyes, when obtained, were very expensive. They too had had their share of casualties and had willingly accepted a Royal Engineers unit being billeted in the Works. There was, however, one positive aspect. The mechanics had devised a new distilling system for cleaning benzene, which ironically made 1915 the most efficient year in the history of the firm.

Perth, from Edinburgh Road, circa 1913

Photograph courtesy of Perth Museum & Art Gallery, Perth & Kinross Council, Scotland

Thomson's Fair City Dyeworks were fairly prosperous due to a workers' 'double-up' system. Garvie and Deas were highly pleased with the boom in dyeing uniforms. Shields' Wallace Works were not so happy. Hoping for a revival in the American market, they struggled to preserve their stocks of flax now that links with Russia had been cut. To do this they were only working a thirty-nine hour week. They were down thirty men and linen yarn costs had risen 100%. Yet, by April, things had improved and full-time working was restored. The year's profits were high, £14,681, and generous holidays were granted to the staff.

Coates' Balhousie Works, however, encountered serious problems. There was the high cost of materials, the fact that twenty-two skilled men had gone off and that the carpet trade had vanished. Short time was the only answer. Then, in April, came demands from the workers for an immediate war bonus. The directors conceded 1s for those with less than 12s a week, 1s 6d with less than 20s and 2s with over 20s. Meanwhile, North British Glassworks (Moncrieff) were doing well making Monax glassware for the Government.

As the year drew to a close, the people of Perth knew that they were engaged in a life-or-death struggle. Change was in the air. Newspapers now had correspondents at the Front and the reportage had a sharpness to it that was different to that of 1914. The poetry had improved: less blood and fire, more a tinge of sadness. There was also a trend to sensationalise crimes and scandals, like the notorious 'Brides in the Baths Murders', on the home front. There was also an awareness that the State now had enough power to play down 'unpleasantness' like the 1st/7th Royal Scots Gretna Green rail disaster or the secrecy about taking photographs. Many suspected that the French had had heavy losses but few knew that the British Army were suffering a monthly casualty rate of 19,000. Even fewer were aware that by December, 512,420 men were casualties and that the war had cost £1,424 million in 1915 alone.

It had been a strange year. There had been some 672 strikes with 2,953,000 days lost and average wage rises of 3s 10d a week. Perth had nothing to match London's hysterical gaiety, but 'Peg O' My Heart' and 'Chu Chin Chow' were popular here too as were many strange fads and crazes, especially the 2s 6d Tea Dansant and the exciting tango. Skirts were much shorter, even knee-length, and many domestics had bravely gone off to munitions. Employers, both private and factory-owners, seemed to be more considerate towards women. But there was still the feeling that Patriotic Barrows were a poor use of women's potential. As for men, there were shorter jackets with breast pockets, wider trousers, fewer turn-ups, knickerbockers and plus-fours. Casual fancy ties were now popular as were officer trench coats with belts and double-yoked shoulders. The social impact of war was easily seen. Match-sellers and bootlace men had gone, and there were far fewer errand boys. Pubs were less popular, whisky weaker and dearer, the GPO was less efficient and trains were often cancelled. Stations, museums and galleries were frequently closed and cars were laid up for the duration of the war. While light reading was none too popular in Perth, there was already talk of '*flappers*' and 'jazz.' It looked like a long war.

Perth Bridge, April 2000

1916

With over 3,770,000 men in the forces, the military were dominant throughout 1916. This was certainly the case in Perth as the Army requisitioned property after property, ruthlessly disrupting the lives of its citizens. As the workload intensified during 1915-1916, the military commandeered the Northern District School for the local pay office as well as School Board houses in Rose Terrace, Atholl Street and Barossa Street. The Old Northern District School, a Red Cross Hospital since 1914, was converted into a recruiting office. Craigend Schoolhouse was also requisitioned, as was Friarton Isolation Hospital which now became exclusively reserved for troops.

Even the Poorhouse was officially pronounced to be a War Hospital and placed in the charge of a Major Paton of the Royal Army Medical Corps who lodged one hundred troops there. Of course, he had a problem: what to do with the inmates? He himself was safely ensconced in the Governor's house, but there was not enough accommodation for his men. He therefore ordered the transfer of all those in the Lunatic Ward to the local asylum. Those unfortunates who had been born in either Ireland or England were returned immediately to their place of birth. Even the dead were dealt with: unclaimed dead in the Poorhouse were sent to Aberdeen Medical School for anatomical purposes.

A measure of army control is seen in the fact that it now controlled no fewer than eighteen hospitals in the Perth Area including Battleby in Redgorton, Aberdalgie and Glenfarg. It was the same with billeting. The military demanded that billeted soldiers have at least 4,300 calories per day, a far healthier diet than that provided by a civilian's 3,859 calories. The calorie intake for troops billeted in Perth was guaranteed by the 'recommended feeding' with five ounces of bread, four ounces of bacon and one pint of tea with milk and sugar for breakfast, followed by dinner consisting of twelve ounces of meat, six ounces of bread and eight ounces of potatoes or vegetables, to be followed by five ounces of bread, two ounces of cheese and one pint of tea with milk and sugar for supper.

Not that army units in Perth were static. In March the Seaforths and the Army Service Corps stationed in Crieff were moved out. In April, the men in the City Halls were relocated in a military camp on the east side of the South Inch. Two hundred soldiers left the Western District School, but had to return when their camp at Scone was flooded. Each crisis in the war, Gallipoli or the Dublin Easter Rising, was followed by a flurry of troop movements.

Scone Camp Military Sports, September 1916

The Army, however, were confronted by numerous problems. They were still short of horses and specialists. For example, Brigadier General Maybury, Chief Engineer of Roads, appealed to the Burgh Surveyor to provide men under fifty, materials, road-scrapers and water carts, for road-making in France. Only two volunteered. Then there was the perennial problem: what to do with bored troops? Here the military were quite inventive. They sent patrols to secure Prohibited Areas like Perth, Abernethy, Aberdalgie, Dunbarney, Kinnoull, Redgorton and Scone. Their instructions were to arrest anyone taking photographs near tunnels or bridges. Others were drafted to local farms for potato lifting, given lectures on Serbia or encouraged to learn Russian or read a book,

Great Britain and the War. All were given talks on temperance and advised to put their money into War Savings rather than spend it on drink.

A more serious dilemma concerned solving the matter of desertions of which there were hundreds. The first sign that a soldier was 'on the run' was the discovery of a uniform concealed in a ditch, buried in a stream or hidden up a tree. Most of these runaways were tinkers. Desperate measures were tried: squads of Military Police scoured the countryside and for anyone foolish enough to help a deserter, it meant six months hard labour.

Like any society the Army had its share of thieves, but what was particularly embarrassing was the small number of commissioned officers who persistently defrauded hoteliers with dud cheques. Over-amorous bigamists and elopements were increasingly common as wartime romances bloomed.

Glasgow prostitutes, with the ever-present threat of VD, who swarmed to Perth were reasonably easy to control. Much more difficult were the hordes of Dundee mill-girls who poured into Perth at the weekends desperate to have a good time. Breaches of the Peace were therefore almost nightly occurrences, especially when regimental rivalry such as that between the Highland Light Infantry and the Black Watch, or a quarrel over a girl, were concerned. With such problems to deal with it was no wonder troops were used every week to assist the police in instructing the populace on air raid drills. But the Army was not without heart. They were genuinely concerned about the growing number of troops who had seen action reporting as 'mentally ill' and the problem of finding employment for discharged soldiers who were severely maimed. The Town Council shared this concern and early in January made plans for such men.

It had long been clear to the Government that the wave of volunteers had dried up and that conscription was the only alternative, no matter how unpopular it might prove. The Army agreed. They knew that the war could only be won in France and large numbers of men were required to win it. Despite the obvious problems involved in training reluctant soldiers, the Army gave its support to conscription. In January, the first Military Service Bill came into operation: all single men and widowers without children, aged eighteen to forty, were called to the colours. Although some have argued that this legislation was responsible for the harshness and stupidity of the Tribunals, it offered a wide range of exemptions including clerics, munitions' workers, sole supporters of dependants, physically unfit and conscientious objectors approved by local Tribunals. Some of these categories were rather vague, 'unfit' for instance, and the Army tried hard to track down the 'physically unfit'. They were not very successful. So much so, that an editorial in the *Constitutional* on 19 January noted: 'Single men are shirking in Perth.' Some were easily caught, two in the Treasurer's Department and two in the Gas Works for example. The Town Council were furious and lodged special appeals with the Central Tribunal in London. Conditional exemptions were increasingly difficult to obtain as the Perth police rounded up shirkers.

By May, phase two had come into operation: the Second Military Service Bill which conscripted all married men and the remaining widowers between eighteen and forty-one. Many saw this as a social revolution and protests poured in, especially from the National Union of Attested Married Men. Still, too many were slipping the net and in August the Manpower Distribution Board was set up to co-ordinate the search. Slowly, the military began to win and by mid-November there were hardly any men left in Perth between the ages of eighteen and forty-one.

One group, the conscientious objectors, continued to irritate the military by repeated refusals to come forward. A steady stream of objectors came through the courts in Perth. The first meeting of the Perth Tribunal was held in the County Buildings on 27 March when forty-three appeals were heard by a court composed of Sheriff Principal Johnston, the Earl of Mansfield, R D Pullar, Martin of Flowerdale and Councillor David Brown. The first forward was a twenty-nine year old dry dyer from the North British Dyeworks and as it was the policy of the firm not to appeal for any of its employees, he lost his case. Another dyer, aged twenty-six, claimed to be morally affronted by the war. He was asked by Captain Watson, the army representative, if he, as a dyer, would refuse to dye khaki uniform. The young dyer saw the trap and replied, 'That is one's economic position.' Watson contemptuously replied, 'It is the safer position at any rate!' The court laughed. Thus ridicule was used, and most effectively, in almost every case.

For the amusement of the readers, all these interviews were reported in detail in the local press. A case in point was that of the Independent Labour Party dyer who appealed as 'a Socialist, a disciple of International Faith and only support of a widowed mother.' This was received with a murmured, 'He doth protest too much,' and howls of laughter. Another dyer piteously described how he supported his mother, only to be told, somewhat callously, 'Use your army pay!'

Such scenes, repeated some 400 times by early April, won the sympathy of the Perth and District Trades and Labour Council. Their dislike of the class-structured nature of the Tribunals was often expressed. Naturally, even within weeks, these Burgh Tribunals were clogged with exemption claims from employers and men with dependants. Many were highly critical of such procedures: Lord Derby, because 160 'starred occupations' were too many, and the Army, because the appellants were clearly 'skulkers and cowards.' A typical view was that young agnostics suddenly converted to a new form of Quakerism that did not require any belief in God, but a belief that the man who would not fight would steal the job of the man who did. Others condemned the Tribunals as inconsistent because exemption was allowed if there was evidence of anti-militarism pre-dating the onset of war. Some deplored the silly questions on exercise and Sunday preoccupation.

Worst of all was the cold logic of the process. A man rejected by the Tribunal was assumed to be in the Army, and if he did not report, he was arrested as a deserter. This was followed by a court-martial and imprisonment with the inevitable rough handling: cuffs; dark cells; bread and water; and force-feeding. Inevitably, it was not long before there were anti-conscription riots. Prominent leaders of anti-conscription groups were soon under general attack, even from the churches, and found themselves either dismissed from their jobs or even jailed. The Army hated criticism from the public and, conscious of the fact that 'conscientious' had never been legally defined, allowed conscientious objectors to serve their time in a civil prison. Even those assessed as 'unfit' suffered badly. They were sent to non-combative duties in

France, digging trenches, erecting barbed wire entanglements, removing mines, bearing stretchers, assignments which were all particularly dangerous, and if their health failed they were not eligible for a pension as it 'had not been caused by fighting.' The aim, clearly, was to punish.

Some justification, however, for the Army's ruthlessness is evident from the casualty figures listed for the Somme in August. In the *Constitutional* on 7 August it was noted that six Black Watch soldiers from the city were killed in action and a further nineteen were wounded. Two days later eight were killed in action, three died of wounds and two were missing while the county lost six in action, three more died of wounds and twenty-two were missing. On 14 August the city lost ten in action, one died of wounds, four were missing and a further thirteen were wounded. From the county the same day, six were killed in action, one died of wounds, four were missing and six were wounded. On 16 August the city lost three in action, four died of wounds, one was missing and three were wounded. In other words, within the space of nine days there were 124 casualties: thirty-nine killed in action, twelve died of wounds, twenty-three missing (mostly dead) and fifty maimed. These figures simply made the Tribunals harder.

Employers were often placed in difficult positions. R D Pullar, for instance, had to abandon his policy of not appealing for his staff. On 13th June he explained his position as follows to the *Perth Courier*. In 1914 he had employed 1,030 men in the North British Dye Works and 357 had gone to war, leaving only 157 of military age. Of these, 138, some 85%, had either attested or were unfit. The remaining 516 were either too young or too old. His appearance at the Tribunal was to save many: his head cashier; clerk; engine/draughtsman; chemist; plumber; boiler attendant; Tulloch Benzine, plant attendant; slater and glazier, the last two being in the firm's Fire Brigade. The first seven, who averaged fifteen years' service were given conditional exemptions, while the last two, younger men, only received three months' exemption. Nevertheless, by September, the firm had 490 in uniform, fifty-two having been called up in just a fortnight. The last two cases R D Pullar fought show the process in a nutshell: a twenty-six year old dyer, a socialist, argued that war was immoral and lost his case! A forty year-old cleaner with eight children to support, was exempted.

None of the above, however, had the slightest effect upon the authorities' war against drink. The average number of drunk and 'incapables' was twenty-eight in January 1914, but by 1916 it was fifty-six. Continually throughout January, there were increases in the cost of drink, such as another 7d on a gallon of whisky. Astonishingly, this had no effect whatsoever, indeed drunkenness rose by 11% in that very month. Nevertheless, the authorities persevered. In February whisky rose again by 3d a bottle. The editor of the *Perth Courier* noted the effect of drink: 'Many soldiers' wives spend their money on wastefulness and love of finery in a mad rush to forget the war.' One case will illustrate: a dyer's finisher, a respectable and skilled worker, was found drunk in a shop, an offence unheard of pre-war. The significant factor was that he paid his 40s fine on the spot.

Not surprisingly, by March, the Central Control Board sought its first convictions. It ordered that no more drink be served in the refreshment room of the General Station on Sundays, while the Chief Constable, again, publicly denounced late-night drinking. Although there were lots of arrests and charges throughout the year, many felt that the Control Board were not sufficiently rigorous. However, they did manage to stop the practice of buying drink for convalescent troops.

Once again, in May, there was a campaign to press for national prohibition and a conference was arranged in Glasgow on 11th May. Meanwhile, it was observed that there had been a considerable increase in the sale of methylated spirits in the city, a large quantity of which was suspected of being sold for drinking purposes. Chemists were urged to refuse suspicious buyers and were warned that sales might have to be regulated. At the same time the problem had reached such dimensions that the Government appointed an Advisory Committee, which included the Oxford philosopher, William McDougall, to examine the matter. Their report revealed, as expected, that more was being spent on drink than on meat and that spending on drink was twice that spent on bread. It claimed that alcohol was a narcotic rather than a stimulant and given that it lacked vitamins, was of small nutritional value and lacked warming qualities. It was not necessary for life and it led to crime, poverty, ill health and industrial inefficiency. The disclosure that London pubs were open some nineteen and a half hours a day, while those in provinces were open eighteen hours, compelled the Advisory Committee to suggest that the former open for a maximum of five and a half hours a day and the latter four and a half hours. The result was the Output of Beer Restriction Act which cut production, diluted spirits and reduced wine imports. The Government would have gone further and bought out the drinks' industry if there had been less opposition and if it had been cheaper. Nevertheless, there were soon State Pubs at Gretna Green, Invergordon and Cromarty.

The Wounded in Perth

It was not only the Army that had problems in 1916. Local government was getting harder every week. Irritating clashes continued with the military over the cost of cleaning up premises evacuated by troops, the priority which soldiers claimed in relation to the use of the city's facilities such as the swimming baths, and the cost of treating 259 troops lodged in Perth Royal Infirmary. The Army paid 2s per day per soldier and when the Town Council protested it was increased to 3s, but this did nothing to cut the standing deficit of £640. Another minor disagreement was over the reduced fares paid by wounded troops on the city's trams and buses which meant loss of revenue at a time when cash was in short supply. There was also a running battle with the Tribunal as a string of skilled men were called up: the water works engineer and the sanitary inspector; the Friarton Gas Works bookkeeper and two from the Town Clerk's office. All of these claimed exemption with the backing of the Town Council. During the Battle of the Somme the numbers increased: two carters in the Cleansing Department; the senior assistant to the City Chamberlain; the inspector of weights and measures; men in the Electrical Department and Electric Station; a gravedigger; the Water Works' plumber; and a driver. Councillors had even less protection and just had to go. By November, there were few conditional exemptions to be had.

Worst of all was the shortage of money caused by claims of employees for war bonuses. Every section of the workforce was demanding rises, the most strident being the carters. Their claim arrived in January and it was not until July that their union, the Scottish Horse and Motormen's Association, founded in 1908, sent their General-Secretary, Hugh Lyon, to fight their corner. He instantly asked for 2s and was given it with a warning that it was 'a last offer.' Lyon reacted furiously. He demanded another 5s or his members would strike and he sent a deputation to intimidate the Town Council. He won another 2s. The same tactics were tried by the gas men. The Town Council pointed out that they had been generous to their colleagues who were in uniform, but the Union of Gas and General Workers called in the Arbitrator who awarded them 2s in April and a further 2d an hour in December due to the great increase in the cost of living. This was the signal for the others: cemetery men, 2s; washhouse and swimming baths men, 2s in war wages and 2s bonus; the lighting department and scavengers, 2s for the former and 1s for the latter; water men, 2s wages and 2s bonus with a day's extra pay per month for the long hours. The last of the early claimants were the janitors and the teachers, the latter receiving £10 bonus. In May there came a second wave of wage demands: the City Hall keeper, 2s; herds on the Inches, 2s; charwomen, 2s; sanitary staff and slaughterhouse men, 2s wages and 2s bonus; and scales of pay were set for all working at the Isolation Hospital. By August a third wave of claims was in operation: the City Chamberlain's office staff; the Burgh Surveyor's staff and the Registrar, to be followed by electricity workers, roads, harbour and museum men who were awarded 2s, and 1s was given to firemen.

It was almost as if there was a conspiracy to destroy local government under a sea of debt and a mountain of regulations. Coal increased in price and Board of Trade pressure finally resulted in the Price of Coal Limitation Act. The cost of air raid insurance continually annoyed the Town Council and they argued strongly that it should be a national responsibility. Planning schedules was a virtual impossibility as the Ministry of Munitions repeatedly asked for the alteration of holiday dates, and the introduction of the Summer Time Act caused real havoc. The whole city was laid out in districts and each was scrupulously searched for scrap metal and wastepaper, while the city's sixty-four byres with their 271 cows had to be inspected. And all of these activities were to be completed by a steadily diminishing workforce. To add to the frustration of municipal headaches were the almost daily applications for flag-days: Russian Jews' Relief Fund; National Life-Boat Institution; Lady Beatty's Navy League; Kitchener Memorial Fund; YMCA; French Red Cross and a host of others. Increasingly the Town Council had to refuse permission and suffer repercussions from bad publicity. Even worse was the enormous rise in the number of war charities which the Town Council bravely denounced 'as far too many in number.'

Then there were the areas over which the State had absolute control, such as the need to extract materials for high explosives from gas. Housing, inevitably, had to be generally neglected; there was neither money, men, nor supplies to maintain them. Unfit houses that rapidly fell into the dangerous category had to be demolished. This was a common feature in the Thimblerow, Skinnergate and Pomarium. To save cash, the Town Council decided not to send any delegates to the Housing and Town Planning Congress in Glasgow.

Transport, a priority area, presented many difficulties, especially after the call-up in January of the last trained tram-driver and the tram manager. Despite the snags, the Town Council, as an experiment, courageously introduced a bus service for schools in February. Staff had to be paid their war wages and bonus as did other employees and they all received 2s in April and a further 2s in December. Convinced that the future lay with the motorbus rather than the tram, the Town Council decided to hire a new type of bus from Edinburgh, somewhat to the annoyance of the ratepayers. Then, in August, came the bad news they had long feared. There was not enough petrol to run a full service. By now, almost anything was possible. After all, one of the tram-drivers was only eighteen years old. Unbelievably, throughout this period of war, a section of the community was still arguing against the running of Sunday trams!

Perth Bridge, circa 1910

Photograph courtesy of Perth Museum & Art Gallery, Perth & Kinross Council, Scotland

Plans for the post-war period ranked high among the Town Council's deliberations, especially after the query from the Under-Secretary of State for Scotland: 'What will be the probable demand for labour on public works at the end of the war?' The Town Council had no difficulty in answering: widen the Glasgow Road bridge, asphalt the streets, find new industries, restore St John's Kirk by removing galleries and partitions and remodel the museum in George Street.

Pensions were a more immediate matter and were growing even more complicated with the introduction of Separation Allowances to military dependants and old age pensioners. The Naval and Military Pensions Act 1916 set up a local pension which was ready by early May.

Essentially, the committee was to consist of twenty-five persons, at least five of whom had to be women and another five representing trades. A further four had to come from either the Soldiers and Sailors Families' Association or the Soldiers' Help Society. The Town Council suggested that seven reflect the trades of dyeing, glass, linen, clothing, shops, bakers and grocers, trades so vital to the community. It was further suggested that three come from the Trades' Council, one of whom should be a woman, and one from each of the following: the Co-operative Women's Guild, Public Health and the School Board. Nominations were for three years, and meeting regularly were: the Lord Provost; two bailies; the treasurer and three councillors for the Town Council; T B Moncrieff of Springlands (glass); F Norie Miller of Cleeve (School Board); a minister; Mrs Calderwood (Newrow); Jessie Dingwall (Trades' Council); Mrs W Smith, Aldie Place (Co-operative Guild); P W Campbell (dyeing); Mrs J J Mackenzie, North Methven Street and Mrs R Smyth, Clyde Place (Soldiers & Sailors Families' Association). Thus, Perth Local Pension Committee actually had more women than suggested by law. Each of these ladies was well known in the city for her strength of character and forceful personality. They were to make their presence felt over the coming months.

Equally important for the community was health and since the Notification of Births (Extension) Act 1915, it was obvious that more attention would have to be paid to the qualifications and training of midwives. The Midwives (Scotland) Act had already decided that their training would have to be much more rigorous. Although concern was expressed for the worrying rise in illegitimacy, malnutrition among children at least, was down. Sadly, little improvement was seen with bad teeth, lice and impetigo. From Murray's Royal Asylum came reports that there was 'less insanity' because 'the community was less introspective and idle.' There was one anomaly: the Society for the Relief of Incurables of Perth and Perthshire, a society for the very poor and the very sick, noted that although their numbers were rising, the death rate had dropped. Since this had first been observed in 1911 it had remained a mystery.

Then there was the problem of venereal disease. The Town Council realised that it was as much a civilian problem as military and they gave whole-hearted support to the recently formed National Society for Combating VD. In November, under Section 78 of the Public Health (Scotland) Act 1897, a Local Government Board set about preparing a local scheme. Finally, the Town Council periodically had to entertain famous personalities who were trying to boost the war effort: Sir Charles B Renshaw, a former Tory MP, Chairman of the Scottish War Savings Committee and of the Caledonian Railway, and Horatio Bottomley, a demagogue and editor of *John Bull*.

For one sector of the community, war had meant a tremendous increase in their workload: the police. Bigamy was now a common offence, as were misuse of aliases, juvenile smoking and wife assault. The police had to cope with an increase in the number of suicides, the problem of housewives turning to prostitution to supplement their drinking-money and a rise in the number of youth gangs. Most policemen resented the current policy of courts to admonish rather than punish and the fact that no delinquent had been whipped in Perth since 1905. Blackout regulations now meant that hundreds were remitted regularly to the Sheriff Court. Then there were the masses of bye-laws which had to be enforced, for example, sheep were not to be driven in the dark through the town.

Legislation continually added to the duties of the police. The Cinematograph Act 1909 called on them to examine fire risks, the Lights on Vehicles (Scotland) Act 1916 declared that 'the inside lights of tram cars and motor buses require to be reduced, shaded or obscured' and the Lights (Scotland) No 1 Order, Defence of the Realm Act (February 1916) insisted that 'all lighting be reduced'. Police even had to assist troops in air raid drill and if there was an air raid, the public had to be warned by a reduction in gas pressure. Experiments showed that while this worked well in the lower areas of the city, Craigie, Bridge of Earn and Scone, it was useless for higher areas like Cherrybank and Upper Craigie. Even more difficult was explaining to the elderly why such blackout rules were needed.

Of course, every fire had to be investigated, especially the February blaze at Lumsden and Mackenzie, Almondbank, which cost £2,000 and the outbreak in April at the Highland Railway Stores, High Street. Sabotage as a possibility figured in almost every investigation. In vivid contrast was the city's insoluble problem of joy-riding cyclists on stolen bikes round and round on the South Inch footpaths! So great was the volume of additional work that Special Constables had to be recruited to follow out the Defence of the Realm Act regulations on pigeons, stop people taking photographs, check begging letters, make sure that shops did not sell books with views of local landmarks, and list all the vehicles in the area.

The Defence of the Realm Act loomed large also in the life of the traditional law agencies. No kites were to be flown in Perth, no petrol bought or sold without permission, no river charts sold and no postcards of Perth displayed. There were serious issues too: searching for escaped enemy prisoners of war in their distinctive 'brown corduroy and blue circle on the back'; tracking down the nineteen pamphlets banned by Regulation 27 of the Defence of the Realm Act such as *Peace at Once* by Clive Bell and *Is Germany Right* by Clifford Allen; distributing circulars on 'What to do if there is an Invasion'; preventing reporters from finding out the condition of Perth Penitentiary's most famous inmate, the Socialist Revolutionary, John Maclean (1879-1923) who was serving three years. It is not surprising that the police asked for and received pay rises in August 1914 and July 1915. In October 1916 they received another 1s 2d and a month later new scales were introduced which gave a sergeant an increase from 37s 11d to 43s 9d and a constable 26s 3d to 36s 9d.

Pay rises were the aim of every section of society. No wonder. Medicines were now up by 25% and fuel was only available for bakers or those engaged in munitions. Domestic consumers found that in order to discourage excessive use, coal also rose by 3s a ton. Even telephone rentals were increased. The editor of the *Perth Courier* caught the feeling rather neatly on 1 August: 'Perth is the city of the lowest wages and the highest prices' as milk, bread, newspapers continued to cost more. As a result of a dull and wet summer, wheat was now 58s 5d a quarter compared to 34s 11d in 1914 and 52s 10d in 1915. The government realised the consequence of this and in October appointed a Royal Commission on Wheat Supplies. But it was in November that there was a sudden rush in price rises: beef from 1s to 1s 8d lb; mutton 1s to 1s 6d; butter 1s 8d to 2s 2d; pork 10s to 14s 6d per stone and a dozen eggs 3s to 3s 6d. Not surprisingly, the City of Perth Co-operative Society demanded that the cost of food needed to be controlled. Prices were now estimated to be up 75% on the 1914 level. The government acted quickly and set up a Committee on Food Supplies, the Board of Trade took over milk supplies, a Royal Commission overlooked sugar and shipping came under the Ship Requisitioning Committee formed in 1915. They also introduced the first war bread composed of husks, potato flour and bean flour or, in other words, adulterated bread.

Not even reports that both France and Germany already had adulterated bread brought any comfort. The wet autumn weather had resulted in a poor potato crop and more and more queues were seen. By December it was clear that sugar, meat, fish and eggs were up between 82% and 173% on the 1914 level. The National Food Economy League advocated porridge and toast for breakfast and scones for tea. With coke now at 23s 4d per ton, it was considered time to create a Ministry of Food and to appoint a Food Controller. Locally the Town Council kept a Register of allotments and encouraged people to grow more. With prices so high, the School Board was compelled to feed 116 children daily at the Cooking Depot where costs continued to rise. Since 1915 potatoes had gone from 2s 9d to 10s; turnips 3s to 4s; carrots 7s to 8s; flour 22s to 27s 6d; white sugar 32s to 42s; brown sugar 32s to 38s; ground rice 16s to 29s; barley 2s 9d to 4s 8d; sago 4s to 4s 8d; currants 5s 10d to 7s; onions 1s 1d to 2s 6d and lentils 25s to 31s. Such rises caused near panic among the city's trades and they responded with a spate of wage claims: painters received an increase of ½d an hour; slaters, 1d; plumbers, 1d and glaziers, ½d. Bakers were granted their demand for 3s on their basic wage of 35s. By October, all trades wanted further increases.

It was the same with business. With 374 of their staff in the Forces, the General Accident Insurance Company decided that there would be no dividend on ordinary shares for the year 1915-1916, while Perth Savings Bank, on the other hand, announced that, as a result of thrift, no less than £1,117,884 had been lodged in 1916.

Meanwhile, the North British Dye Works admitted that there had been 'a considerable diminution' in their trade, especially in cleaning fine dress for entertaining and the cleaning of household goods. But at least, all the staff were still at work, although on short time. Few of the public realised that the firm's motor vehicles had been confiscated by the Army and those that they occasionally saw in the city had only been hired. Even fewer knew that the Engineering Department produced munitions and that mechanics made shells. R D Pullar, now rarely in Perth, was normally at Huddersfield supervising the extraction of benzol, toluol, carbolic, sulphuric and nitric acids, the common links between dyes and explosives. Meanwhile, the North British Dye Works steadily lost more men to the Army. By mid-January some 293 men were serving with thirty-two units: ninety-four Black Watch; fifty-one Army Service Corps and twenty-three Scottish Horse. Four of them were already dead. By the time a full working week had been restored, R D Pullar had retired as President of the Society of Dyers and Colourists at Bradford, having served his two years, and his son, Lt J L Pullar, had been invalided home from France.

So many girls in the North British Dye Works were engaged in voluntary war work that the *Perthshire Advertiser* wrote about 'Pullars at the Front.' One of their weekend ploys was to scour the hills around Perth searching for lichens and berries to replace dyes. According to some there were at least eighty such plants available in Scotland. Girls in the Tailoring Department adopted British prisoners of war in Germany and acted as pen pals for the lonely. By June, even these were compelled to lodge a wage claim to meet the rise in the cost of living. The firm responded with an immediate 2s to 3s per man and 1s to 1s 9d for women and boys. To their surprise the workers said it was not enough. Then, when R D Pullar was at the Annual Congress of the Society of the Chemical Industry in Edinburgh, news arrived that 50,000 English dyers had just been given war increases. The staff at once requested the aid of the Board of Trade and the Government to acquire the same, but their claim was rejected. With the whole community plunged into gloom with the casualty lists from the Somme and the workforce steadily demoralised, R D Pullar granted an immediate bonus of 4s to men and 2s 8d to all others, which meant that each man had had a rise of 7s within three months and each woman 4s 8d.

This increased the firm's outlay and the lack of petrol forced the directors to cancel all Works' charabanc outings. By September some 409 of the employees were serving the colours and the press joke of

'The Pullar Battalion' became a reality. Just as the editor of the *Perthshire Advertiser* was warning that the future threat to Perth would come from America rather than Germany, the Amalgamated Society of Dyers, Bleachers, Finishers and Kindred Trades demanded a rise of 10s for men and 6s for women by 24 November under threat of strike. While the *Perthshire Advertiser* described the situation as 'alarming' the editor of the *Perth Courier* perceptively warned 'After the War - Problems with Trade Unions'. In general the press were not in sympathy with the union demands considering that the men at the dye-works had had a rise 'considerably more than many sections of the working population.'

P and P Campbell were in a happier situation. By sheer luck they had always used British dyes rather than German and they therefore invested heavily in the new firm, British Dyes Limited. Despite the fact that there was a small Royal Engineers' unit billeted in the Works and that all their male employees were attested under the Derby Scheme, they were suddenly faced with the call-up of some of their key staff. It was made worse in July when the general manager, the Edinburgh district manager, and the residential engineer were called up. Fortunately the manager, Leonard Rigg, was able to persuade the City Tribunal to grant conditional exemption. It was even harder in September when the foreman carpet-cleaner, the foreman dyer, the calender man and a dyer's finisher were all called up. The latter had to go to the Army, but the others were given two months' grace. When Rigg was recalled in October to plead for the foreman dyer he told the Tribunal that the firm had once had sixteen dyers. Now only eight were left and they were all foremen dyeing khaki. Seventy-five men were already in uniform.

When he returned, a fortnight later, only two dyers were left: 'If we lose these qualified dyers the doors of the Works will close - forever!' The *Perthshire Advertiser* took up the matter on 14 November: 'Perth Dye works in danger - Campbells losing too many skilled men.' The Board of Trade issued a statement admitting concern, while the press posed the crucial question: 'Is dyeing an essential trade?' Rigg's last appearance before the Tribunal in 1916 saved the calender man with a simple plea: 'He is the only one left who can work the machine!'

At Thomson's Fair City Dyeworks, the situation was quite different. Although they too had felt the effects of war they had cleverly moved their resources into laundry work which was doing well. Advertising a 'hygienic laundry' with collars and shirts a speciality, they were actually making money. Shields' Wallace Works was having 'a perplexing time' and many of their looms were idle. But they too had diversified from linen to cotton and although they still worked a fifty-one hour week, stores of flax and yarn were nearing exhaustion. Their problems were much the same as faced by other Perth industries, but they still turned in a healthy profit of £16,881 despite the death of their chairman, Mr Leitch, and the return of the two shell-shocked directors, Lt A G Shields and Lt G Shields. They warned the Tribunal: 'If more men go then the Wallace Works may close.' At Coates' Balhousie Works, rising costs resulted in severe problems. Although they made blankets for the Forces, thirty-seven of their best men had been called up and the remaining thirty had all attested. Some employers in Perth were complaining about the level of income tax, 1s in the £, and urging the setting up of a Federation of British Industry to match the trade unions. Others, like the Caledonian Railway Workshops, were using their war-profits to upgrade their equipment, in this case, by introducing electric lighting.

Amidst all this gloom it was important to keep up the nation's morale. In the earlier part of the year, this was done by subtle handling of events in the newspapers. For instance, much was made of the food riots in Dusseldorf and Berlin in the summer of 1916. Equally, the death of Lord Kitchener, Secretary of State for War, produced 'overwhelming feelings of regret and sorrow' in Perth. Then there was the feeling in July that with Lloyd George as the new War Secretary things might improve. In November, with the re-election of President Woodrow Wilson in the USA, many hoped that America would soon enter the war. There was still an irrational obsession with spies: consequently there were no weather reports or chess problems in the newspapers, no public clocks allowed to chime, no whistling for cans.

Songs proved to be particularly uplifting at this time. Among those popular were: 'Keep the Home Fires Burning'; 'It's a Long Way to Tipperary'; 'Peg o' My Heart'; 'If you were the only girl in the world and I was the only boy'; 'There's a long, long trail awinding into the land of my dreams'; 'Pack up your troubles in your old kit bag and smile, smile, smile'.

Slowly, literary propaganda gave way to films. In 1916 there were five cinemas in Perth: the BB in Victoria Street; the High Street and City Hall cinemas; La Scala in Scott Street and The King's in South Methven Street. Throughout the year they did a roaring trade with war films, while spy stories were especially popular. The Government did not mind as they helped recruiting and even the better educated were drawn to enjoy this comparatively new visual experience. The desire for escapism was universal and the filmmakers responded with more comfortable cinemas, longer films, more serials and the cult of stars like Chaplin. Deliberately attacking the pre-war image of 'coarse', and bowing to the Entertainment Tax, filmmaking rapidly developed into an industry, exploring animated cartoons, faking battle scenes for the *Battle of the Somme*, dramatically adapting famous novels into photo plays and analysing class differences and sex problems in such epics as *The Loveless Marriage*. That these techniques were successful is shown by society's continued positive response to the war. Twenty-four members of staff at Murray's Royal Asylum, twenty-nine members of the School Board, 376 former pupils of Caledonian Road School, 196 from the Northern District School, 181 from the Western District School, 161 from the Southern District School, sixty-five from Cherrybank School and seventeen from tiny Craigend School had all gone off to war.

Those at home had not flagged either. They gave comforts to the 6th Black Watch Battalion, entertained the wounded, maintained school gardens, knitted for the War Guild, helped out at Soldiers' Clubs, collected medical bottles and sphagnum moss, and invested in War Savings. Their sense of service is shown by the Wylie family of Perth and their seven soldier-sons: one in the Canadian Division; one in the Canadian RAMC; two in the Machine-Gun Corps; one in the Royal Dragoons; one in the Army Service Corps and one in the West Kents.

Some sections of the community irritated the majority. Perth had long since become disillusioned with their guests, the Belgians, especially as they were refusing to register and were costing the city 6s 4d each per week. With seventy of them in Perth, that meant £22 3s 4d a week or £1,152 per annum. Even news that some of the Belgian soldiers in the area were only thirteen years old did not win them sympathy. Police kept a close eye on some whom they suspected of 'shirking.' Twenty-two were considered eligible for military service and were tracked down. Among them were: Francois Junius, goods packer; Charles Verlegen, gardener; Reny Broos, bottle packer and Gerard van Leempuuen, jam maker.

The Labour Party was also regarded in 1916 with a mild degree of suspicion. After all, members preferred to discuss the prospects of rail nationalization rather than the war, and spent too much time trying to acquire seats for their members on the Town Council. Worse was their campaign for the release of John MacLean from prison and their lectures on 'War is a threat to the working classes.'

As 1916 drew to a close, certain aspects of the war became clearer. Women were obviously not being used to their full potential and many felt that it was not enough to attend cookery lessons and sell flags for good causes. They were certainly making progress, however slowly. Most job-applicants in Perth were now women, there were more female nurses at Murray Royal Asylum, more women wanted to teach physical training and the Army Pay Corps were training some women to be clerks. Many young women, especially domestics, were thrilled to hear that their services were wanted in munitions and on the land. But they still had enemies, namely, farmers and trade unionists who warned that there would be trouble with female clerks, thousands of whom worked on the railways. There was also a growing sense of confidence among women with the news that Lord Northcliffe was now in favour of the female franchise.

Obvious too in 1916 was that the power of the State was increasing and had to increase further. With five new Ministries: Pensions; Labour; Food; Shipping and Air, the State now controlled rail, shipping, coal, iron, wool, food, agriculture and munitions. The cost was high with considerable bureaucratic rules, an omnipresent Defence of the Realm Act and intrusion on personal rights. But there were benefits too: the extension of Unemployment Insurance; the issue of War Savings Certificates for small investors; and the belief that with the Lloyd George Coalition and the five-man Cabinet, the nation, at last, had a chance of winning the war. The people knew that the cost would be great in both men and in money, but it would be worth it. There were even mysteries which the all-seeing economists could not explain. Why, although there were as many as sixteen pawnbrokers in Perth, was the number of vagrants falling? Why had unemployment virtually disappeared? Why had real wages gone up? The man in the street did not care. He was, as the Government knew only too well, too war-weary to bother. He just wanted to see an end to the war.

John MacLean, Peterhead, 9 May 1916

1917

It was the third year of the war, a year which the people of Perth were long to remember as 'the worst year of the war.' No longer were the Army and its needs paramount in their thoughts. Now it was personal survival in a society racked with industrial bitterness and on the verge of civil disorder.

The appointment of a Food Controller in January was a clear indication of just how serious the food shortages and rising prices were. As a result, food economy posters flooded the country. The *Constitutional* admitted that the nation's food was increasingly monotonous and advised the growing of herbs as 'useful for adding taste.' Even children from Perth Academy were growing vegetables in front of the school in Rose Terrace. Nobody could really explain why commodities were so expensive, but is was reckoned that the cost of living in Perth since August 1914, had risen by 89% and was still rising by at least 2%-5% per month. When London introduced a food coupon scheme, the local press in Perth showed an interest. Ironically, the cost of dying had also mounted as funeral costs soared.

The School Board realised the need to cutback and ordered 'strict economies' in books, stationery, apparatus, fuel, light and cleaning. Indeed, so desperate was the situation, that the Town Council ordered the Chief Constable to release from duty any man who had experience of farm work. Some sixteen came forward and they were used as advisers to 'food-growing groups' all over the city. They also toured schools and encouraged pupils to become involved in food and hygiene courses. Children were even known to skip school and slip down to the harbour to collect potatoes and vegetables spilt during unloading from coastal vessels. Not that there were many ships in dock. Germany's proclaimed 'unrestricted U-boat warfare' saw to that. Foreign ships with food rarely came even though at this time the UK imported 100% of its sugar, tea and chocolate, 80% of cheese, 79% of cereals, 73% of fruit, 65% of butter, 51% of eggs and margarine and 36% of vegetables.

April 1917 earned the title 'crisis month' as food became extremely scarce in the city. In the Poorhouse, for example, sugar was a thing of the past and the inmates did their bit by setting up a piggery and using every part of the grounds for potatoes. About this time, the London coupon system was extended to all parts of the country for meat, tea and butter. Queues were even longer than in 1916, meat was almost impossible to find and feeding pigeons was banned. There was even a rumour in Perth that the troops at Scone had to endure bad food as well.

By now the Government realised that some form of rationing was inescapable. After all, France had meatless days and it was generally known that Germany used 'crow meat', only one egg every three weeks and that shops had to close at 7 p.m. Rationing had even been considered as 'a war possibility' as far back as 1903 and was the subject of a Royal Commission Report in 1905. Nonetheless, the thought was not accepted with any enthusiasm as its inauguration would openly signal to the enemy the success of its U-boat campaign. This mattered little to the man in the street who could not understand how a 4lb loaf could cost 1s 1d, nor could he accept the fact that the highly publicised Food Economy Campaign was a shambles. Neither could the Town Council, and they furiously debated the eternal questions: who was responsible and what could be done? A measure of the near panic, which the authorities strove hard to conceal, was that tinkers from all over the area were flocking into Perth, abandoning their traditional summer sites and squatting in the slums of the Thimblerow. This was risky given the frequent searches by the military for deserters and the police for shirkers. So many were hiding in this derelict area that they captured the sympathy of the Duchess of Atholl who urged the setting up of a committee to help them.

By high summer, the Ministry of Food had begun to ration sugar, butter, lard, meat, tea and cheese through coupons and cards. Unfortunately, they omitted to stipulate prices and blatant profiteering quickly ensued. 'Profiteer' was a word with a fearsome, emotive power, which could unleash the most passionate hatreds. The Town Council shared this reaction and argued that the recent rise in the price of bread 'was not excused by the bakers' pay rise and is not an accepted reason.' Although bread was not rationed it was strongly suspected in the city that beans were being added to what the citizens contemptuously referred to as 'the dark war bread.' Bacon was now 1s 8d and tea was 4s per pound. This persuaded the Government to launch a campaign to encourage tea-drinkers to switch to cocoa which was only 7½d per quarter when sold loose and 'went quite well with oats for breakfast.' At the same time gardeners were urged 'to live off their vegetable plot' and 'enjoy Sunday teas outdoors.' For children, sulking because their comics had just doubled in price, the Government proclaimed that there was nothing better than 'regular intake of rice pudding, liquorice and cod liver oil.' As for hotels, two days a week without potatoes and one day a week without meat was 'healthy'. Perth School Board struggled mightily to offer nutritious fare: lentil soup with ground rice pudding on Monday; mince and potatoes with boiled stew and corn flour pudding on Tuesday; and fish, potatoes and baked treacle on Friday. By August, it was calculated that the average family in the UK was spending 39s a week on food. It was hardly surprising. Wheat was now at the astronomical level of 75s 9d a quarter.

Soon the Food Control Commission and merchants, following interminable disagreements, agreed to a rationing scheme. Because the fixed price of bread had to be at least 1s, the government was forced to add a subsidy and the result was 'Government Bread.' In Perth, it was simply called 'the cheap loaf.' Fortunately, autumn brought help for pensioners with the introduction of better Separation Allowances for soldiers' wives. The payment for a child below the age of fourteen was now 23s. If there were four children then 40s 6d would be paid. Private soldiers' widows received 13s 9d, while the widows of junior officers were given 40s. Both received, in addition, a third of that sum for a boy up to the age of eighteen and a girl to the age of twenty-one. There were also disability pensions. Health insurance was automatic for troops and there were maternity benefits for wives. Most people agreed that clothing was costly and this helped to put an end to knickerbockers, while tobacco rose by an excruciating 70%. Indeed, it was estimated that the basic survival level for the average family was 15s a week for food,

1s 10d for fuel and 4s for clothing and other items, a total of 21s per week.

Sadly, in Perth many did not earn anything like this and it was to prove to be the fuse for civic disorder. The Town Council, knowing that trouble was brewing, could do little. They had enough on their hands struggling with bread orders and the fact that 'the best parlour coal' was now 34s a ton, while 'the best nuts' were 28s a ton. With the mid-October wage rise for miners, the situation worsened: coal rose by another 2s 6d a ton. In general, this meant a further 2s more per week for the average family in Perth. The local coal committee appreciated this, but were more concerned with the effect of the increase on the very poor, particularly as winter was drawing near.

Not many were aware that the city had fewer than 600 tons of coal in stock. In the streets of Perth morale reached a new low as people queued for hours, often unsuccessfully, outside empty shops. It was clear to all that even voluntary rationing had failed. Coal was soon rationed and a Cheese Order and a subsidy on potatoes were introduced. With December came the National Rationing Scheme for sugar, and while some complained, others had the good sense to realise that people in London were much worse off. There, a whole range of foodstuffs was almost impossible to obtain: sugar, tea, butter, lard, margarine, dripping, milk, bacon, pork, condensed milk, rice, currants, raisins, spirits and Australian wines.

While all these changes were swirling through society the Town Council were manfully doing their best to encourage the citizens to grow food. Public parks were being ploughed up all over the land. Potatoes were planted even in Wellshill Cemetery and allotments were laid out at Jeanfield. Pigs were fashionable and lands near the Smallpox Hospital and the swimming baths were all cultivated. Craigie Knowes was next on the schedule and nearby residents were given free supplies of cabbage plants and seed potatoes. Then, in rapid succession came Viewlands Place, Rose Crescent, Windsor Terrace, Queen Street, Feus Road, Park Place and Athollbank. All of these were developed in conjunction with the Food Economy campaign organised by the Food Controller, William Asher, the city's sanitary inspector, whose duties as such earned him another £30 per annum.

William Asher had a lot to do. He had to find ploughmen to show how to cultivate the soil, organise cookery demonstrations in the City Hall, supervise livestock and find new areas for cultivation. Craigie Golf Course, three fields at Pitheavllis, Pickletullum, Goodlyburn and Gallows Road were soon made available. Naturally, he needed support and a Food Control Committee of twelve was established which included a representative from labour, representatives from the two city wards, and one female. Their Food Control orders carried the full sanction of the law and by then Asher arranged for cows to graze on the two Inches and to begin the cultivation of Moncrieffe Island Golf Course.

As one might expect, the workers did not stand by to see their standard of living disintegrate with the rise in prices. They fought back with wage demands. Among the first to do so were the members of the Amalgamated Union of Co-operative and Commercial Employees and Allied Workers (AUCE) at the Co-operative Society. They demanded a war bonus in late January. The directors had just awarded them a rise of 1s a week which they refused. Simpson, the AUCE organiser, came to Perth and at a meeting of the 300 Co-op employees asked for recognition of their trade union. There was no response. At the Annual General Meeting of the Perth branch of the AUCE the Co-op directors were described as 'tyrannical'. Alarmed by the bad publicity which was widely exposed in the press, the directors immediately conceded 2s, but not through the AUCE. The union struck back claiming that the Board of Directors of the Co-op Society were mostly non trade-unionists and that 264 of the 357 employees earned under 20s weekly. They proudly rejected the 2s. This caused consternation in the Perth Trades' Council, but they condemned the 'brutish tactics' of the AUCE. Simpson was immune to criticism and pressed on trying to enrol as many assistants, milliners and dressmakers as he could.

Plumbers were next. In 1914 they had 9½d an hour, advanced by 1d an hour war bonus in January 1916 and then ½d an hour in February 1917. That meant that they now earned 11d an hour, but they wanted 11½d. Teachers pressed for their war bonus of £4-£5 which they were granted in March, followed by a scale to £80 per annum in October. Janitors supported them and they were given 2s 6d weekly. In

May the bakers demanded a colossal 7s a week increase. As they had already won two rises of 2s and 3s their masters decided to offer them only 4s. The bakers retaliated with a threat to strike in May. This was enough for the masters to give way and they conceded 5s which immediately forced up the cost of a loaf.

Bread was now 1s 1d a loaf. In September the bakers threatened strike action again and the masters settled quickly. The highest paid tradesmen in Perth were the printers. In 1913 their wage was 32s 6d and in thirty months they had wrestled no less than 13s 6d from their employers. With 46s they still were not satisfied and demanded another 4s to make 50s a week. This aroused anger among the public and envy among the other unions. Even more annoying was their published statement of 3 June 1917 that they were opposed to the employment of women in their trade. The least selfish group were the engineers in the Amalgamated Engineering Union. At a protest meeting held in late January, they were more interested in the quality of housing in Perth for workers than their own pay packets. At a similar meeting, a month later, they suggested that unions should merge for greater strength and unity. Throughout this period, trades' militancy was increasing and Marxism was clearly spreading.

The group of workers who caused the most trouble for the Town Council was the National Union of Gas Workers. Rattled by the Ministry of Munitions' Leaving Certificate HM14 that 'workmen employed in the Gas Undertaking would further be subject to the Provisions of Part 1 of the Munitions of War Act 1915, which prohibits strikes and lock-outs,' they were not satisfied by the 2s rise recently given. Their secretary, J Mackenzie, argued that they wanted an increase of wages and not a war bonus which could be taken away at the pleasure of the Council. He further suggested that if the Town Council disagreed, they should call in the Arbiter. They refused to do so, simply saying: 'It's a war wage rather than an increase.' To make their point they openly refused rises to the gas manager and a female in the showroom. A month later, when the gas workers and meter men wanted a rise, Mackenzie was careful to claim 8s 'founded on awards granted.' The Town Council stalled for time and Mackenzie warned them that if the Arbiter came, he would be awarded at least 4s.

Still the Town Council refused to call in the Arbiter and the union reminded them that as they came under the Munitions of War Act, they were obliged to call him. Finally, when Sir James Urquhart was appointed Arbiter, he awarded 3s to all in late September. This aroused great dissatisfaction and there were protests. When the gas collectors were subsequently denied a rise, a mass meeting of the National Union of General Workers was called for 29 December at the gas works with meter and gas fitting men, street sweepers, firemen, lighting, work and paving employees, at which they decided to strike as a protest against the Town Council and its rejection of their 8s claim. As the strike was to take place on 3 January 1918, the Town Council asked the Minister of Munitions for advice and they then held a special meeting. The carters too were restless and announced that their formidable leader, Hugh Lyon, was coming to Perth to argue their case. It was not until May that his argument was presented. Other burghs having awarded carters between 4s and 5s a week extra, he wanted an additional 1s a day for his men. In June they received 3s, but were not pleased and the issue went to arbitration. In November he asked for 20s on the pre-war rate and time and a half for overtime. They were awarded another 4s, but were again dissatisfied and threatened to strike on 10 December. The Town Council ignored them. They did not strike, but once more requested the judgement of the Arbiter.

The scavengers were nearly as much trouble. In May they demanded a rise and three months later were given 2s. By that time there had been another surge in the cost of living and they wanted a further 6s. The Town Council were still debating this claim when, near the end of the year, the scavengers lodged yet another wage demand for an extra 2s, making a total of 8s.

Every other group of workers employed by the Town Council followed the lead of these unions and lodged their demands. In January, five female cleaners received 2s war bonus. In April a demand came in from Mill Street and Canal Street washhouses. In October the police demanded 8s and a month later were granted 5s. As the last request had horrified the authorities, they were quick to award senior officers new scales in November. In June the watermen tentatively asked for a war bonus, but by the end of the year they were claiming 8s. The bell-ringer also submitted a claim in June. Firemen had requested a rise, but when nothing was done, some quit the trade union. The rest were quickly granted 7s but three days later they were back for more. The most difficult group in June were the electricity men. Eight of them received war wages of 2s, but instantly demanded a rise in their basic rate and were offered 4s. When they discovered that their colleagues in other cities had been granted 12s, they petitioned for the same sum and for an Arbiter. Both claims were rejected and the issue of electricity workers in a gas plant coming under the Munitions' Act was raised. The eight workers then threatened mass resignation, but were again refused. To the astonishment of all, they demanded a further 10s. A few days later the *Perthshire Advertiser* ran a column headed 'They Must be Joking!' However, the Arbiter, Sir Richard Lodge, arrived in October and awarded 5s, but with the warning that 'the compulsory payment of war wages, 12½% on earnings, shall not alter or become part of their time rates.'

Town Council plumbers in June received 3s to 4s in war bonuses. In July roadmen asked for more but were not granted their 3s until the end of the year. The Inches men asked for a rise in July; and the paviors who were awarded 1s in August demanded another 8s a few months later. October saw many other claims: lighting men received 1s; switchboard attendants, 3s; fitters 2s to 5s and joiners, 7s. Then cemetery men were granted 3s in December. Even the white-collar staff on whom the Town Council thought they could rely for support constantly pressed for increases. In January, £20 a year was awarded to the senior lady clerk in the City Chamberlain's office, 4s to a clerkess with the Town Clerk, 4s to three in the City Chamberlain's office (two female), 2s to two in the Burgh Surveyor's office (one female), 2s for nine men and 1s for six females in the Gas Treasurer's Office and finally, 2s to five men and 1s to four females in the Gas Department. Senior staff working for the Town Council were careful to have their increases added to their salary rather than recorded as a war bonus. The second assistant to the City Chamberlain received £20 as a salary increase rather than a war bonus. The demands for increases did not work for all however. In October, when the lady clerks of the gas office who asked for another 6s were refused, they all resigned. Such a wide range of rises throughout society raised wages by some 30% in 1917 alone.

But it was in the industrial sector that the real crisis would come. North British Dye Works had survived an exceedingly difficult year in 1916. Trade had fallen, costs of dyestuffs, coal, and packing materials had all risen and delays in rail transit had been equally damaging. Some 40% of the male staff had gone and the reduction in the number of mechanics was a troublesome factor. A steady stream of decorations and casualty lists continued throughout the year. The decision of the Arbiter, Sir Thomas Munro, against ten leading dye firms on 9 December 1916 in Glasgow was regarded as a tremendous victory for the Amalgamated Society of Dyers, Bleachers, Finishers and Kindred Trades. Briefly, this meant a rise of 8s per week to all time-workers over eighteen years, with 5s to youths and girls, 22½% to piece-workers earning under 35s, 17½% to piece-workers earning between 35s and 45s, and 15½% to those above 45s.

In rapid succession all the major firms, except John Pullar and Sons, accepted and paid out this war wage. A gauntlet had been flung at the feet of the union and they would most certainly pick it up. On 30 April, William Rushworth, General Secretary, demanded 10s a week 'over pre-war rates due to the enormous increase in the price of food-stuffs - in order to live above starvation level. Your workers have become the lowest paid workers in Scotland.' The firm's reply was curt. The rise would add £60,000 per annum to their wage bill without any increase in production. At the same time they strenuously denied the charge that they were employing cheap labour on starvation wages. The union cleverly applied pressure on the Association of Master Dyers and Cleaners in Scotland in order to isolate Pullars.

Meanwhile, the union organised a crowded and lively rally in the City Hall on Friday, 8 June, which the press described as 'The rising of the dye workers!' There were five speakers: Councillor David Bruce, foreman baker in the Co-operative Society and President of the Perth Trades' Council; Mrs Jessie Jardine, a young war-widow from Alexandria, Vale of Leven, who worked at the Turkey Red Company; John Teevin, from Lennoxtown, Chairman of the Glasgow District Council of the Dyers' Union; Hugh Sinclair, gas worker and J M Rae,

Secretary of Perth Trades' Council. Bruce claimed that the wage demand was for a war wage and as there were now 600 dyers in Perth 'we must be organised!' Mrs Jardine spoke of her meagre 11s a week until the union obtained 7s for women and 11s for men as a war bonus. She mocked the Pullars' argument of rising costs: 'I do not believe they pay much more than they did before the war for their dyestuffs and still they plead poverty every time!' She went further: 'If you get a costume or a suit dyed today, you have to pay double the 1914 price for it. Where does the difference, the profit, go? To the worker? No fear! We would not get a penny out of it but for the trade unions. We in the dyeing trade know what the work costs, we know that, after all, dyestuffs are not so greatly increased. But we do know that the charges for our work are about doubled, and what we want now is better wages, better conditions and shorter hours. We don't want a strike!' Teevin told how, in pre-union days, girls in Glasgow only gained 6s a week, while he, as a dyer, only had 18s 4d for a fifty-six hour stint. 'Now, thanks to the trade union, girls in Glasgow, under eighteen years, have 14s.' He reminded his listeners: 'Sir Thomas Munro said there should be a 7s war bonus for women and 11s for men. Your employers say they cannot give you a rise, but you are being bluffed! You are the people making profits and surely the day has gone when you had no say? Join the Union, now!' While Hugh Sinclair confirmed that 'Perth is a dear place', Rae reminded the audience that 'all twenty-three trades in the Trades' Council had given rises of 4s to 5s since 1914 with one trade having three rises in just a year.' A committee was then elected. By the time a second mass meeting was held on Thursday, 14 June, there were 1,000 in the Dyers' Union.

Once again, Bruce and Mrs Jardine urged the 1,500 in the City Hall to enlist in the union at once. This time Rushworth spoke. He recalled the struggle to establish a dyers' union in Perth between 1911-1912 and described how, in Glasgow, he had won rises of 12s for girls, while in Perth the highest rise, for bakers, was only 5s. He admitted that Pullars had been a good firm, but, 'There is more profit being made now in dyeing and cleaning than in any trade in Scotland. Capital has no conscience. The employer is only concerned as to what profit he is gong to get. Why do men get 30s and women 16s for the same work? This will have to be sorted out after the war.' Sinclair added his piece by commenting on the high TB rate in the city and the fact that wages had only risen by 5% while food costs had risen by 98%. Rae finished the meeting with a rousing cry: 'Non-unionist labour is a menace to the workers' liberty!' That night, Rushworth asked for an Arbiter, while the editor of the *Perthshire Advertiser* reflected: 'These are extraordinary demands, but Unions cannot be ignored in 1917.'

The firm's directors objected to 'the harmful agitation' and pointed out that they had not uplifted any salaries since 1916 and had, indeed, lost a substantial part of their capital, a fact which they could prove if the union examined their books. While the *Perthshire Advertiser* on 19 June observed that 'dyeing is not a fortune-making trade', the editor, a week later, made a sensible comment: 'Perth as a city is deeply, too deeply for its own good many think ... closely connected with the dyeing industry ... a very large proportion of the city workers now find themselves at the edge of the precipice whither they have been brought by the one industry dependence of Perth. They are shackled to a trade which is, in its essentials, a non-productive one.' Other commentators noted that freight charges in the city had risen by 12½%, while raw cotton had gone up from 5d to 1s 7d.

On Thursday, 21 June, yet another meeting was held in the City Hall attended by another 1,500. The usual speakers were there - Bruce, Rushworth, Simpson, Mrs Jardine, Rae and Mr Farquhar of the NUR. Bruce began with a denunciation of the fact that some of the girls in Pullars only received 13s and he urged Government to subsidise wages during the war. Simpson demanded that the milliners and dressmakers of Perth be organised, and finished with the ominous: 'We want non-unionists cleared out of the dyeworks in Perth once and for all!' But it was Rushworth that people had come to hear. In Glasgow, one firm had given all its employees a war bonus of 6s. Even P and P Campbell had given 1s to 4s in bonuses, but not Pullars. They had rejected a claim in 1915 and could do the same again. He proposed a two-month trial period with a 10% rise to all workers and if business fell by 10%, then the rises would be returned. If the directors refused, he proposed meeting the trade union in open debate before the citizens of Perth. He scorned a Pullars' advertisement: 'We have been working for no profit throughout the war.' He finished with the mocking comment: 'So there's no point looking at their books!'

Rushworth was nothing if not inventive. He soon wrote again to the directors suggesting that a small war tax be placed on all goods to be used exclusively for increased wages to workers. He was convinced that when customers were told of this they would gladly pay. If, after three months, it were found to be detrimental to the firm, it would cease. The alternative was simple: arbitration. The editor of the *Perthshire Advertiser* realised the significance of this challenge: 'Perth is a city on the brink of an industrial war' it claimed. Yet again, the firm dismissed the proposals as 'commercially impracticable'. They had already given rises in December 1915 and again in December 1916, not to mention the generous allowances given to soldiers' dependants.

Meanwhile union leaders had written again to the Employers' Association of the Dyeing and Cleaning Trade of Scotland asking for a conference. As a precaution, they had also given H J Nelson, Chief Industrial Commissioners' Department, Whitehall, the statutory twenty-one days' warning that a dispute was imminent. They also wrote to the firm, as required by the Defence of the Realm Act and the Munitions' Act, giving seven days' warning. The editor of the *Perthshire Advertiser* caught the air of panic on 7 July: 'Dyers' Strike Imminent: A Fight to the Finish. For the first time in the existence of labour in this Perth industry, the wages problem has ceased to be local and has become a British trade dispute.' For the first time 1,400 members in the Perth branch of the Dyers' Union would collect strike pay.

For some unexplained reason, the Board of Trade delayed their reply and the union again took the initiative on Wednesday, 18 July when they summoned their fourth rally in the City Hall with an even larger crowd of 2,000. Again there were the familiar figures: Rushworth, Mrs Jardine, Rae, Munro of the NUR and Beaton of the Shop Assistants' Union. Mrs Jardine spoke of the need for munitions' work in Perth, while Beaton announced that Edinburgh's dressmakers had just won a rise. Once again, however, it was Rushworth they wanted to hear. He told the audience that the Masters' Association had refused to negotiate and that Pullars had rejected his claim three times. He pointed out the anomalies: the lowest paid, unskilled female in Glasgow earned 19s, but a skilled twenty year old in Pullars only had 16s and those younger than twenty, 13s. Yet 1lb of butter cost 2s 2d and a loaf was 1s 6d 'and for this they work from 6 a.m to 5 p.m - for a 1lb of butter, a dozen eggs and a loaf! How do they pay the rent? The pre-war £ is now worth only 3s 6d. Even the traditional sweated industries have 16s 9d to 22s a week now. 90% of workers at Pullars are in the union, but those at Tulloch are afraid of losing their houses. You have not joined the union for a bit of fun. I have been in fourteen strikes and I have won fourteen times!' He then issued a ballot paper which read: 'Repeated efforts have been made by my trade union officials with a view to convincing you of the justice of my claim for increased wages during this abnormal period through which we are passing. Such efforts, unfortunately, have failed meantime. I am, therefore, compelled to adopt the only course now open to me, if I am to safeguard my right to live. I therefore tender to you seven days' notice that I shall terminate my employment as from the above date (1 August 1917).' As the union were anxious to avoid a showdown at a special meeting on 24 July in the Labour Rooms, they asked for a delay in handing in ballots while they went to London to see the Board of Trade.

Near the end of July the union turned its attention to P and P Campbell. The firm responded with a statement that their workers were satisfied because they had been given a rise in June, always had overtime and never suffered deduction when slack. As for their enrolment in the Dyers' Union, they were convinced that their workers had been 'induced to join.' This aroused the interest of the *Perthshire Advertiser* and on 21 July they published 'the facts' - that the average female wage in Campbells and in Pullars was only 16s for twenty year olds and just 12s to 13s for younger employees

Panicking, Campbells' directors posted a notice, an 'Appeal to Workers' to think carefully before signing any ballot. They indicated that if trade were lost it would never return. If the North British Dye Works closed, workers would have to go and work in the munitions' area and this would cease with the end of the war. They urged workers to wait for the judgement of the Board of Trade, because they paid above union rates. Both Campbells' and Pullars' workers delayed the submission of their notices just as the news broke that the Dyers' Union had now established itself at Luncarty Bleach Works with 150 members.

August began with a show of trade union strength and solidarity when 1,000 NUR men marched through the city to the North Inch where they were joined by 1,000 dye workers and 2,000 others to hear Robert Smillie, President of the British Miners' Federation, and John Marchbank of the NUR. Campbells' directors responded with a clear warning that if the Works closed for any reason, 102 men would be called up.

Then, on Saturday, 18 August, 681 at Pullars and 211 at Campbells, 892 in all, handed in their notice. Pullars were still refusing to negotiate and Campbells were threatening to close down. On 21 August, the *Perthshire Advertiser* led with the headline: 'Perth Strike Sensation - Will Dyeing Industry be Paralysed?' Still, Campbells had not given up. On Tuesday 22 August, they revealed in the *Perthshire Advertiser* details of their lowest and highest advances: dyers, 5s 9d; cleaners, 6s to 8s 3d; looking-over staff, 2s to 7s; pickers, 5s to 6s; despatch room, 4s to 8s 9d; sewers, 2s to 9s; stenters, 2s to 12s; feathers, 2s to 3s; dressmakers, 3s to 8s; milliners, 2s 4d to 4s; upholsterers, 2s 4d to 5s; tailoresses, 6s to 7s; male French cleaners, 7s 5d to 9s 3d; female French cleaners, 4s to 9s; pressers, 3s 10d to 8s; hats, 5s to 9s; framers, 2s to 3s 6d; male glazers, 3s 6d to 7s 6d; female glazers, 4s to 6s; white ironers, 2s to 8s, plus, if the rises were under 5s, 2s would be granted immediately and if over 5s, then 1s immediately.

The directors also offered 'to meet a large and representative gathering' on Wednesday in the Glazing Room. On Wednesday, 22 August crowds of workers circled both Campbells and Pullars crying, 'We want to work through the union!' which made Pullars' directors post a notice to the effect that they were 'operating at a heavy loss' and had already 'granted advances late in 1915 and 1916.' Consequently, they would not need fortnightly workers after 6 September, nor weekly after 1 September, after which workers could then 're-engage.' This forced Perth Trades' Council to hold 'a hasty meeting' at which it was agreed to lodge a strong protest against the Board of Trade and report them to the Minister of Labour. Further, a committee of twelve was appointed in case of a strike and the Co-op Society asked 'to come forward with material help, such as augmenting the Union allowance.' Then came a bombshell on Friday, 24 August. After a frank discussion Campbells and the Dyers' Union had reached agreement. There would be no strike and both would go to arbitration. This came as a surprise to Pullars who now posted another notice: 50% of the workers (31% men and 60% women) had tendered notices and the firm wanted 'a new agreement'. They warned that there would be pickets, but the doors would open at 12 noon on Tuesday, 24 August. Although there would be no steam or power, there would be plenty to do. However, if intimidated, they were to go home, write an account of what had happened, and they would be paid. That night the union 'in a demonstrative mood' hired the Co-op Hall to hear Rushworth, Bruce, Mrs Jardine and James Taylor, President of the Perth branch of the Dyers' Union, warn their members that 'a fight is coming.' Rushworth, just back from London, made a scathing attack on Pullars' proposal of 'wages only to those who blackleg.' He condemned the directors as 'autocratic' and told the workers not to accept their insurance cards.

On Saturday, 25 August, work stopped. R D Pullar sped south to the Minister of Labour with his Reconstruction Proposals: a forty-eight hour week, starting at 6.30 a.m, full-time for all, and a bonus scheme. The *Perthshire Advertiser* sadly commented on 'The first real crisis in the history of dyeing in Perth' and asked, 'Is the fabric of the country's diligence to be ruthlessly torn down?' On Monday 27 August word spread that R D Pullar had been summoned to London and as it was a public holiday hundreds marched to the North Inch and the same evening 2,000 gathered in the City Hall. Bruce thrilled his audience by telling them that the NUR were ready to join them in the strike and that was the reason R D Pullar had been called away. 'Tomorrow,' he said, 'will be the Battle of the Gates - it will be your Bannockburn!' Sime, of the Jute and Textile Workers' Union, Dundee, told of his union's fight with Cox and Company: 'You have to teach Pullars the lesson we had to teach Cox in 1911.' Taylor was more down to earth. He reminded them that the Finishing Department used to have bonuses at 12s, but after three months it was 8s and finally 4s. 'Bonuses mean Blood Money! We should have an eight hour day and 8s a day!' By now almost all the workers wanted everything run by the union. Finally, Rushworth spoke of the year 1913 when Pullars and Campbells agreed to pay 16s a week to girls of eighteen, yet Campbells had only done so in the last six months. He condemned Pullars' new proposals as 'half-thought out and needing too many supervisors ... the bonus system is the curse of the trade ... a brutally scientific method of piece-work by an employer to get twelve hours' work out of a person in nine hours!'

Although it rained on Tuesday, 28 August, pickets were out at Tulloch before 6 a.m to prevent the entry of workers loyal to the firm. At 8 a.m they marched to Perth to find that the eight gates of the North British Dye Works were covered by the police. Then about one hundred loyalists appeared and the striking females became hysterical, despite the attempts of union officials to quieten them down. Coats were torn, police slapped, police helmets lost, all of which was witnessed by the directors from their windows. At 9 a.m they closed the Works and the loyalists went home to catcalls and howls of derision. The strikers gathered at the Co-op Hall at 11 a.m and marched back to Kinnoull Street to demand their 'lying-time.' This was refused. They then marched to Tulloch and then back to Perth. That afternoon they assembled on the North Inch to hear Taylor and Rushworth plead for 'peaceful tactics.' The editor of the *Perthshire Advertiser* on Wednesday, 29 August, described Perth as 'a city under a black, industrial cloud.' It was certainly noisy as strikers paraded the streets banging empty tins before they returned to the Works to request their money once more. Again it was refused and they marched pointlessly to Tulloch and back.

That weekend 3,000 watched the local sports, while A E Pullar accompanied his brother, R D Pullar, to Inverness. Coincidentally, that weekend Perth's sugar supplies finally ran out and the Co-op sacked their foreman pastry baker, Councillor Bruce. The *Perthshire Advertiser* asked the question on everyone's lips: 'Could it be victimisation?' The bakers thought so and threatened to strike. Late on Friday, 31 August, one hundred loyalists sneaked into the warehouse to deal with urgent orders.

'Hope for Settlement' was the *Perthshire Advertiser*'s headline on Saturday, 1 September, as they published Pullars proposals for a settlement: a forty-eight hour week, 6.30 a.m to 9 a.m, followed by breakfast from 10 a.m to 1 p.m and dinner from 2 p.m to 5 p.m. These hours would begin on Monday, 17 September. Work would finish at 1 p.m on Saturdays. Those who did not like these arrangements could work a 43½ hour week from 8.45 a.m to 1 p.m and 2 p.m to 5.30 p.m. Employment would be full-time and there would be a bonus system. Workers were asked to elect a committee of men and women to assist the directors prepare new pay scales which would apply from 5 September. As was to be expected, people noticed that there was no mention of the Dyers' Union. Ironically, that afternoon, a strikers' parade was led by a Charlie Chaplin imitator.

By Tuesday, 4 September, 'the air in Perth was electric'. Police detachments from Forfarshire and Dundee had been marching to the police station and rumour had it that forty, mounted Lanarkshire police had ridden out of the railway station. At an evening meeting in the Co-op Hall the new proposals were rejected 'because there was no mention of the Union' and at 7 p.m about 800 people who assembled on the South Inch were led by the NUR. Brass bands paraded the streets to the cheers of thousands. By 8 p.m strikers were filing into the City Hall where Taylor, Bruce, Rae, Mrs Jardine, Sinclair and Rushworth awaited them.

Taylor talked of strong support from Glasgow. Bruce reminded his listeners that Pullars had 'sabotaged' efforts by the Manchester Union of Dyers in 1877. Rae denied that there was any outside agitation in the strike. Sinclair declared that 'he would rather be a hooligan than a blackleg!' and all assembled sang 'Sandy Dewar's Strike Song.' Rushworth was next. He warned them that Pullars were trying to starve them back to work. 'But help is flooding in. Strike pay can be doubled! Messrs Pullars and the police must remember this: we are not a deteriorated little remnant of the Trade Union Army, we are a regular part of the great Trade Union Army of Britain!' He scorned the Pullars' visit to Inverness: 'They can go to Monte Carlo if they wish!' He reported that the union had paid out 10s strike money to men and 5s to women and that cheques had come in from business men in Perth, the NUR and bakers. Taylor caught the fighting mood of the meeting: 'Tomorrow will be fought our Waterloo!' They then streamed out into the streets and sang and paraded until midnight.

The Battle of the Gates became a reality on Wednesday, 5 September. Some loyalists managed to sneak into the Works at 3 a.m, while groups of strikers went to loyalists' houses uttering threats and howling abuse. One was even grabbed and locked in his cellar. By 5.30 a.m, while it was still dark, sixty-five police arrived at the North British Dye Works just before a very large crowd gathered at the corner of Mill Street/Kinnoull Street to greet each approaching loyalist with shouts of 'Blackleg!' Most, after 'some pretty rough handling' turned for home. Four women had their hats torn off and one manager needed no less than twelve hefty constables to help him fight his way into the factory. One loyalist did not make it; he collapsed and was taken seriously ill.

By 6 a.m, 'the crowd was enormous and aggressive,' booing, hissing and jostling the police, especially the 500 near the Main Gate. Suddenly three Lanarkshire mounted police galloped up Mill Street only to find the mob had formed a cordon of some 2,000 across the street. By then, twenty-four female loyalists who had become part of the mob were 'jeered at by hilarious girls' and deliberately jostled by the young men in the crowd. One policeman seized his assailant and flung him to the ground. The mob became infuriated and blows were exchanged with the police as the scene of disorderliness continued. Missiles of fruit-skins, apples, stones, old shoes, rings, oily waste and even iron punches were flung at the horsemen. One struck a sergeant's horse and it darted into the crowd. There was a mad scramble for safety amid the turmoil of screaming women. At least four people were knocked down.

So serious had the situation become that Chief Constable Scott summoned the trade union leaders and asked them 'to restrain their supporters.' Accordingly, Taylor appealed for 'no rowdyism' and Rushworth urged 'a peaceful solution'. Nevertheless, both denounced the use of horses. When they begged the strikers to disperse, they did so reluctantly. By 8 a.m, they were back. This time their aim was to block the entrance to the warehouse and clerical staff offices. Again there were scenes of pandemonium and fighting as one clerk was felled and a clerkess fainted. For almost an hour the mob seethed to and fro in a seesaw battle with the police. Scott ordered the arrests of four youths and a woman.

The management had had enough. Work was stopped at 9 a.m and those loyalists who had gained entry went home pursued by baying demonstrators. By 10 a.m, the huge crowd was led by one hundred NUR men. There was another arrest as more missiles were thrown. Then, at 11 a.m, the mob surged towards the Co-op Hall to hear Taylor denounce the Chief Constable for the use of horses and warned that if they were not withdrawn he would call for a general strike. The same afternoon there was a parade to the North Inch to hear speeches from Taylor, Bruce, and Rushworth who claimed that only one hundred loyalists had got to work and all had left early.

That night there was a mass rally to the South Inch and a mile-long procession threaded its way through the city with brass bands, fluttering union banners, and a song, 'If it wasn't for the gallant little Union, where would the dyeworks be?' The *Perthshire Advertiser* commented on its 'catchy refrain'.

Later that evening, the police told the Chief Constable that they would draw their batons the next day. Things were clearly getting out of hand and it was obvious that lives might well be lost. Scott went at once to Sheriff-Principal Wilson KC who summoned more mounted police, and together they roused James Taylor from his bed. Taylor agreed to keep the peace and he told the NUR men to stay away. Scott and Wilson then requested R D Pullar to close the Works.

The following day, 6 September, at 5 a.m, notices were posted at Perth and Tulloch advising loyalists to stay at home as the Works were closed. One thousand strikers who had gathered by 6 a.m, soon mutilated the notices as Taylor proclaimed a union victory. By 6.30 a.m the area was strangely quiet. But at 9 a.m, the crowds assembled outside the Burgh Police Court where a former Pullars' employee, twenty-four year old Jessie Peddie of Burt's Close, was charged with intimidation under the Conspiracy and Protection of Property Act. She had attempted to prevent Robert Wilkie, the manager of the Postal Department, from entering his lawful place of business. She pled not guilty, was bailed at £5 and remitted to the Sheriff-Principal. Margaret Barty or Robertson was next. An ironer from the High Street, she was charged with assault on PC Clark of Perth by slapping him. Found guilty, she was fined £1. When she left the Burgh Court she was cheered and applauded by the huge crowd outside. That evening the Dyers' Union held a Victory Dance in the Co-op Hall.

Next day, the strikers held a picnic at Buckie Braes while J M Rae wrote to A F Whyte MP complaining about the use of police which had led to a riot. Another letter was sent to the Secretary of the Parliamentary Committee of the Trades Union Congress in Blackpool asking for help. The *Perthshire Advertiser* commented: 'Recent events are most distressing and in the silence of the great Works it is almost eerie ... there are a plethora of go-betweens, while hundreds roam the streets, idle.' The editorial was to the point: 'Let us have more of a human touch, as in the old days, and mindful of changing conditions, less of the vanity which precedes a fall or the violence which alienates sympathy and brings its own nemesis.'

Both sides had time to reflect. The loyalists' thoughts were with their colleague, John Elder, a dye-worker, who had taken ill in the scrimmage and had just died. He had worked in Pullars for almost twenty-seven years. The union too must have paused for breath. They had kept their promise of 10s strike pay to every man and 7s to every woman striker, but it had cost them £400. Suddenly, there was stalemate: R D Pullar, ill with 'a serious nervous breakdown' had gone to Inverness for a rest. On Monday, 10 September, the strikers had a picnic at Almondbank as the weather was fine. Meanwhile six appeared in the Burgh Court and, to the astonishment of the public, it was revealed that only two of them were in the union. Four, part of a 'riotous mob', were charged with assault on Margaret McLeod, clerkess and Anne Harris, feather dresser. The four were: Andrew Martin, a dyer's labourer; David Smith, an apprentice moulder; Frank Scrimgeour, an apprentice fitter; and William McCall, an apprentice dyer. Bail was set at £5 and they were remitted to the Sheriff Court. Then seventeen year-old Agnes Bell, a mill worker at Coates, pled not guilty to knocking the cap off Donald Chisholm, aged seventy-three, a dyers' finisher. Bail was set at £5. Lastly, George Dunn, a NUR signal lamp man, was charged with obstructing inspector Kirk of the Hamilton police and was bailed at £10.

Two days later, it was announced that Sir James Urquhart of Dundee was to be Arbiter in the Campbells *vs* Dyers' Union dispute. For some dyers it was too late. They had moved to other towns, convinced that the Pullars would never employ them again. A few had joined Campbells. However, industrial unrest is infectious and other sectors were soon disgruntled: John Shields and Company; the Wallace Works; Messrs Coates Limited; and the Spinners and Manufacturers, Balhousie Works. Their workers gathered on the evening of 15 September to hear Hugh Sinclair declare: 'Until you are organised and have a voice in the conditions of your labour, you will continue to have grievances and no remedy.' Rushworth, tired and not at his best, simply condemned 'unscrupulous profiteers in the war.' John C Henry from Brechin Mill Factory Operatives criticised the nine-hour day at Shields and the ten hours at Coates, while J F Syme of Dundee Textiles, observed that 'all reformers are agitators in history!' They then resolved to demand a 10s rise, that war bonuses be paid as part of wages and that overtime should be at double rate. Rumours that A E Pullar and union officials were in London to see the Minister of Labour, and that the Duke of Atholl had offered to arbitrate, were confirmed. Management could select six loyalist representatives and the workers could also select six who could be members of the Dyers' Union.

Suddenly, the harmony dissolved when notices were posted on Monday, 17 September, announcing that Pullars 'would re-open under the old conditions on Wednesday, 19 September at 10 a.m.' The *Constitutional* reported that it was a bombshell to the workers. Instantly the air was filled with bitter condemnation of the union and according to the *Perthshire Advertiser* the workers were furious and felt betrayed. Behind the scenes there was a flurry of discussions. Mrs Jardine and Rushworth were at the City Chambers discussing a solution with McCash and Hunter, solicitors for Pullars, while the entire strike committee went to the Station Hotel to see the Duke of Atholl.

That evening, at 7 p.m in the Co-op Hall, the workers were told that negotiations had dragged on for seven hours. With little discussion, the firm's offer was rejected and the dispute was now to go officially to *avizandum*. The strikers were not pleased and were hostile to their leaders. When the strike committee suggested that in the meantime they should all go back to work, there was a chilly silence. The only positive feature was the Duke's assurance that Pullars would agree to his judgement and that there would be a conference at 11 a.m on Monday, 24 September. But to the union officials' horror, the strikers absolutely refused to obey.

Only Rushworth could save the day: 'We have won two great points - arbitration and recognition of the Union. The Duke will allow the whole strike committee to be present and the committee needs two female members and will pay strike pay on Saturday. Remember, your employers are autocrats. They have originated from a bygone age. They are still living in times one hundred years ago when the employer was entitled to own the machinery and the men and the women inside the Works. You have got to break that down. You will break it down by reasoning, not by bludgeoning and pistoling.' Still not convinced, sullen and resentful, they dispersed.

The crowd gathered early on Wednesday, 19 September, and 'showed great reluctance to enter the Works' and some did not enter at all. Concern was expressed over R D Pullar's health, but A E Pullar curtly replied that 'the illness is not linked to the strike troubles.' That night, at the age of fifty-six, R D Pullar died in an Edinburgh Nursing Home, his son, R M Pullar, by his side.

An excellent chemist, R D Pullar was regarded by his contemporaries as clever and cultivated. He had held a wide range of voluntary offices in the city he loved. At a private funeral, a few days after his death, he was described as 'a man of kindly acts and great determination and wonderful enthusiasms - wise and judicious, with strong convictions, absolute integrity and indomitable energy.'

Although stunned, both management and workers decided to carry on and the Station Hotel conference, chaired by the Duke of Atholl, opened at 11 a.m on Monday, 24 September. Those present included A E Pullar, two directors and three non-unionists, a Dyers' Union official, Hayhurst and five unionists. Ten other unionists were spectators in a 'generally friendly discussion.' After a vote of condolence to Mrs R D Pullar, her brother-in-law, A E Pullar, announced formally that he intended selling the North British Dye Works and if no buyer was forthcoming, he would close the Works down. Thus any settlement could not be binding on any buyer. It was agreed to meet again on Thursday, 27 September. A E Pullar then gave a rambling, defensive statement and Hayhurst passed no comment.

The *Constitutional* declared: 'A Bombshell on Perth!' in their headline of 26 September. Everybody knew that if the North British Dye Works closed, 2,000 jobs would go and the effect on the city would be catastrophic. The firm's annual wage bill was in the region of £150,000, not to mention cash given to pensioners and the relatives of 430 men in the Army. Then there would be the loss in rates followed by far higher rates for others. As the implications dawned on the citizens, there was near panic. Some realised it had nothing to do with the war, but rather ever-increasing competition and the geographical isolation of Perth. Even the Perth Trades' Council lost its composure and appealed to Dundee Trades' Council for aid. The rebuff was sharp: 'The Dyers' Union is very wealthy and the application is ridiculous!'

By now everyone was emotionally drained and amid feelings of guilt and apprehension, a settlement was soon reached at the next meeting: 5s 'emergency bonus' for those with less than 38s a week and eighteen years of age or more; 4s to women over eighteen; 3s if under eighteen, and all would be paid from 19 September, but only by the present management.

For years the scars of bitterness remained between loyalist and striker. The Pullar family felt betrayed and the workers were changing. The days of long-serving craftsmen, priding themselves on being with a family firm, were over, for good.

On Saturday, 29 September the charges against the two women arrested were dismissed and it was not until 17 October that the five young men went to trial. It was long and exhausting, lasting seven-and-a-half hours. The defence argued that the charge was invalid as the accused were arrested at different times and could not, therefore, have been part of a mob. One was acquitted and the others were fined £15, £10, £5 and £1 respectively. Only Campbells problem remained to be resolved and on 8 October, Urquhart's Report was released. He flatly rejected the demand for 10s 'because Campbells' had introduced a scale for men in October 1913 and one for women in April 1914.' By August 1914, most women were on a higher rate than the scale, while the men 'were either well above or well below.' He indicated that there had been many rises during the war, some automatic according to the scale, some on merit and some due to the war. Thus there would be no general rise. Since 1 August 1914 the average rises for a fifty-one hour week were 3s 6d for journeymen dyers, 4s 7d for wet cleaners, glaziers and finishers, and 2s 10d for females. But from 1915-1917, the firm was unprofitable. 'Still,' said Urquhart, 'pre-war wages were too low.' Therefore, he gave 4s to journeymen dyers, 3s to men over eighteen, 2s to boys under eighteen, 3s to women earning 14s a week or more, 2s to other women and 10% to piece workers. There was to be no change in overtime and the existing bonus of 1s a week (paid half-yearly) would be added to wages and paid weekly. He warned that 'All of these are temporary increases of remuneration, intended to assist in meeting the increased cost of living and are to be recognised as due to the existence of abnormal conditions prevailing in consequence of the war.'

The *Perthshire Advertiser* editorial hailed the awards as 'bold and generous' and showing a somewhat sympathetic leaning 'to *demos* as the rises will cost at least £5,000.' It was generally believed that the story could not end there, because by the end of the year there was an enormous increase in the cost of dyes, cleaning agents, coal and labour and there were no improvements to the plant.

The other factories in Perth had all suffered during this traumatic year. In mid-October, the Luncarty Bleachers, Messrs James Burt-Marshall Ltd, sold out to Manchester Bleachers Company. At P and P Campbell there had been more dyes available in 1916 than in 1915 due to Swiss sales and the Royal Navy's capture of German dye stocks, but shortage of skilled labour meant possible closure. One director, Peter Campbell, and 70% of the men were in the Army, despite the fact that the firm had huge army orders. Leonard Rigg was constantly appearing before the City Tribunal to save his men.

At the Shields and Company Wallace Works, there were problems as well. In 1914, 181 men were employed, but by 1916 there were only 101 left and only twenty-three of these were of military age. Even the females were down by 170 and many looms were idle. Although there had been an increase in exports to the USA, no Russian flax was available for production. Irish flax had risen three times in price since 1914 and cotton yarn was also dearer. Still, profits in May, basically from damasks, were very good at £24,065. Of the eighty-four men in 1914 of military age, there were now only twenty and there were no power-loom operatives left. The Pullars' unrest had spread to Shields in September and by 3 November, employees were demanding rises in line with other linen workers. Two weeks later, an award of 4s for men, 3s for women and 1s 6d for all under eighteen was made. But the managing director, H J Shields, dramatically refused to give this national award, as recommended by the Arbiter, because he was not a member of the Employers' Association. Legally, he was right and the union had slipped-up badly. Desperately, they tried to correct their mistake by writing to Appelton, Secretary of the General Federation of Trade Unions and to Sir George Askwith, the Arbiter, as well as Mr Henry, President of the Scottish Textile Council.

Meanwhile, Coates Balhousie Works found themselves in a welter of rising costs. The year 1916 had been a good year with huge orders from the War Department for sandbags, twines and blankets. Now, however, fifty men were in the Army and even though wages had been raised in April and November, the Pullars' affair made their workers increasingly restless. Thomson's Fair City Dyeworks had been hit hard in 1916, with the exception of the laundry which did well with Voluntary Aid Detachment and hospital orders. Then, in January 1917, came disaster for the 150 female staff: 'a disastrous conflagration' totally destroyed the dyeworks. Fortunately, the Pullars' Fire Brigade saved the laundry. Still, the damage was estimated at £15,000, not to mention loss from theft. John Moncrieff Glass Works added an extension as they sought to meet Government orders, but Perth Bakery Company went into liquidation as flour had become too scarce. At the harbour, all the sheds were empty and the owner pleaded with the Town Council to allow him half-rents.

Amidst all this confusion the Army was still active. With over 4,250,000 men and women in uniform, their presence was felt everywhere. In Perth, the Army Pay Corps had priority for games on the North Inch, while maimed troops were given work in the Caledonian Workshops. The Black Watch requested the City Hall for their concerts and a Royal Engineers' unit requisitioned Shield's Motor Garage. Of course, the Army had its problems too: even soldiers had had to be awarded a pay rise of 6d and deserters were proving an insoluble difficulty. There was still a search for horses and there were social embarrassments like soldiers on leave finding their wives and mothers under arrest for drunkenness.

More alarming was the growing concern for the mental health of troops who had seen action in France. Murthly War Hospital was prepared as a sanctuary for them as was a section of the Murray's Royal Asylum. Sadly, some escaped and drowned themselves in the Tay, while others were regarded as 'lunatic-deserters.' Others claimed to be ill and simply refused to return to their duties. 'War and the incidence of insanity' together with the 'Treatment of mentally deranged soldiers' became popular topics for medical study. Murray's Asylum itself was puzzled by the fact that it had 157 civilian patients, the highest number since its inception in 1865. Doctors wondered if this increase was due to a greater willingness to accept mental treatment or to the stress of war. Recruiting, of course, went on remorselessly. In January, Pullars had appealed on behalf of their last slater and glazier and a forty year-old clerk. By March every male teacher in Perth under the age of thirty-one with an 'A' or 'B1' call-up grade received their call, and as the war machine continued to absorb more and more men, the question of dyeing being 'an unessential trade' was debated. Both Campbells and the Trade Council continually appealed to retain their key workers with little hope of success, especially when families like the Pearsons could boast of having nine sons in uniform.

Excessive drinking was still a national threat. Indeed, by May, it was calculated that drink, in the period 1914-1917, had absorbed 4,400,000 tons of grain and 340,000 tons of sugar, all brought to the UK at the cost of seamen's lives. This vast amount of cargo was equivalent to bread for the entire nation for forty-three weeks and sugar for thirty-three weeks. Not surprisingly, 2,000,000 people petitioned the Government for an end to the drink trade for the duration of the war. Although output was cut, pubs rationed and a strong temperance movement evolving, the Government still felt that prohibition would shatter morale. After all, an increase in the price of a pint to 8d had led to riots. In Perth itself, the Central Control Board fought a losing battle, especially against farmers who drank heavily at Hay's Market.

With ninety-three drink-sellers licensed for the city, social problems such as drunken mothers, cruel husbands, and neglected children were unavoidable. Convictions carried little weight. Even the Volunteer Review by the Duke of Connaught was marred by drink, and a prohibition drive led by Annie S Swan in the City Hall was useless. As for the police, they firmly believed that the fault lay with the Central Control Board's reluctance to prosecute more rigorously. Consequently, drink-related crime was undiminished with reckless motoring, joyriding on stolen motorbikes and driving without lights. Juveniles were as bad. The wild boys of Perth skipped school, broke windows and stole.

Not that the police had the time or the resources to cope with them. They were too busy catching bigamists, checking itinerant musicians to see if they were deserters and chasing escaped prisoners of war. Escapes were now more common. Several enemy soldiers employed in farm work broke out of the camp at Auchterarder. Two in particular caused a lot of bother: Karl Konig and Daniel Schneider fled from their camp at Kinlochleven and were finally caught in Rannoch Wood. In addition there were more usual duties to deal with. A £12,000 fire broke out at Pitcairnfield Bleach Works and another at Moncrieff Glass Works. There was a build-up of ice on the Tay, and there were summer drownings and investigations into whether or not Lumsden and Mackenzie had poisoned the river.

Aliens still had to be supervised: Dutch, Hungarians, Norwegians and Americans. There was even a Russian, Nicolai Schwartz, at Invergowrie, who, because of his name aroused great suspicion. Some people wanted to treat the aliens with kindness. Sir James Ramsay of Bamff, near Alyth, wanted to offer a home to nineteen-year-old Fritz Somerkamp, a student at Cambridge University, but because the student was also a Berliner, the request was refused. There were countless human hardships. Henry Rasche, a German living in Perth, had no money, his wife was an alcoholic and he had four children to support and Isidore Cohen, an Ottoman, wanted to come to Perth to study, but was rejected. Worst of all was the plight of Scots girls married to aliens. What category were they in?

The Belgians were still unpopular, mainly because they lived off the generosity of the Pullars and had insisted that they be assessed as a war charity. Three Belgians left Perth because they felt they were badly treated and to some extent, this was true. Certainly, the police disliked them simply because they could not spell curious names like Declereq. The last straw for most people came in November when the Belgian community appealed against the assessments on houses at Numbers 2 and 4 Rose Terrace, 29 Kirkgate and 42 Main Street. And yet they only paid water rates!

Perhaps the Town Council bore the greatest strain in 1917, hounded as they were by a pack of troubles. The worst of these was the never-ending spiral of costs. Air raid insurance and practice drills all cost money and there were plenty of these, especially after the men of the Perthshire Volunteer Regiment were sent on 'permanent observation'. Some even thought the expenditure was worthwhile when an airship was reported over Perth. Eventually, when the annual premium reached £72 18s 4d, the Town Council refused to pay and the public agreed with them.

Fire insurance rates were no better, but School Board outlays were even higher. For instance, the cost of meals in 1912 was £97, but by 1917 this was up to £537, while the £44 expenditure on boots in 1912 had now become £119. Workmen's insurance was up because of the Workmen's Compensation (War Addition) Act 1917, and there was a huge number of pensions to be provided for. The twenty-seven men and women on the Pensions' Committee, seven of whom were required to represent labour, had their hands full all year. Separation allowances were a headache, while soldiers' pleas for aid were heartache. Then there was the annual deficit from Perth Royal Infirmary which was rising steadily as annual costs soared to £11,813. The Army's allowance of 4s per soldier per day for 788 wounded was no solution. Even the Pullars' strike had been expensive with the cost of twenty police from Lanark, seven from Forfar, eight from Dundee, not to mention others from Bridge of Earn, Crieff and Blairgowrie. Wastepaper and scrap-iron still had to be collected and it was almost impossible to acquire a motor wagon for the city's refuse. Flag-days continued to be commonplace, especially for Limbless Sailors and Soldiers and for Navy and Army Workers, while arranging War Loans and trying to recruit gravediggers was another thankless task. One particular difficulty was operating the

Retail Coal Prices Order 1917 and keeping an eye on coal-merchants' profits, while trying to persuade the Gas Works to produce more tar.

Then there was health. It was in 1917 that the authorities fully realised that venereal disease was indeed 'The scourge of the world' with most of the troops in hospital its victims. From every side came disturbing data. Quacks were causing enormous distress with their 'magic remedies' and even the Murray Royal Asylum reported more syphilis cases than ever.

Perth Royal Infirmary introduced VD treatment and laid aside four beds for sufferers: two male and two female. In April the Medical Officer drafted a scheme and a Special Committee was set up to study the reports of the Royal Commission of Venereal Disease and the Public Health (VD) Regulations (Scotland) Act 1916 with a view to devising future plans.

As for children, there was a growing realisation that the nation had a vested interest in their welfare. Thus more free boots were distributed, the first school oculist was appointed, a holiday home for needy children was opened in Pitlochry, a health visitor was appointed in August and the Health Centre in Princes Street, which catered for 177 mothers monthly, was declared 'a great success.' Far more children were now being vaccinated, numbers rising from three in 1907 to 299 in 1916.

But there were mysteries as well. Was the birth rate falling simply because so many men were away? Was the high death rate among incurables and the insane simply due to food shortages? Was there something sinister in the fact that only 56% of births were registered under the Notification of Births Act 1907? Why were there so many regular epidemics of diarrhoea, ringworm and rickets?

Another growing conviction concerned the need to improve housing by the elimination of slums. Bad housing and high rents obviously sapped communal will and the State began to appreciate that some form of subsidised housing was inevitable after the war. Already there were attempts to calculate post-war working-class housing needs and house factors were asked to estimate costs. This they did. The sum of £10,000 would be required just to improve housing in the city. Even in the darkest days of 1917, thought was given to the causes of poverty in an industrial society, while the Ministry of Reconstruction prepared plans for a demobilisation scheme. Everything was covered: unemployment; nursing; law; education; transport; materials and scientific research. Locally, there were discussions on sites for war relics, methods of assessing war damage and locations for new industries. Then, at a more immediate level, there was discussion on such questions as whether higher fares should be introduced to pay conductors in the city's transport scheme, whether females should be employed at a lower rate and whether gas propelled vehicles should be hired. The Council simply put up parcel rates and converted one bus to gas!

Meal Vennel, circa 1930

Photograph courtesy of Perth Museum & Art Gallery, Perth & Kinross Council, Scotland

Despite all the hardships suffered by the citizens of Perth throughout 1917, the vast majority of them tried to carry on with their support for the war. Children helped to make sandbags and gathered chestnuts for dyes; elderly ladies still knitted assiduously or served early morning teas in the railway station; and the Allies' Grand Fancy Fair was well-supported. While women cooked and served meals in the Soldiers' and Sailors' Club in George Street, their men folk enlisted in the National Service Volunteers. In March the National Service Campaign Committee was set up consisting of the two political agents in Perth, one Trades' Council representative, the former Dean of Guild, two councillors, one member of the Chamber of Commerce, five clergymen, one solicitor and the three newspaper owners. By June, a support organisation, the Perth Motor Volunteer Corps appeared and they soon purchased a Belhaven ES863 and a Commer ES632 for emergencies.

Little else changed. Lady Burghclere's Prisoners' Fund, patriotic concerts in the City Hall, the War-Dressings Organisation, the Patriotic Barrow Fund, Our Own Men Fund, entertainment for convalescent troops and subscriptions to the War Loan Movement, all continued as before.

Much of the patriotism owed a lot to newspapers and propaganda. Together they magnified the captures of Baghdad and Jerusalem, the entry of the US into the war and the use of tanks at Cambrai. At the same time they played down the Bolshevik Revolution, the failure of Nivelles's Push, Passchendaele, the collapse of Italy, while the Treaty of Brest, Litovsk and Messines were, naturally, 'victories.' There was, however, a growing distrust of the printed word and the feeling that the State, under the clever direction of Perth-born John Buchan, Director of Information, just played with words. This cynicism spread. Fortune-telling was more important to many than orthodox religion, marriage was less popular and many solved their domestic problems by simply running off.

This mood of uncertainty was obvious in politics. A Co-operative Party had emerged in 1917, as had a National Party under dissident Tories. Even Arthur Henderson had left the War Cabinet because he thought it was time for peace. Perth Trades' Council had now abandoned their Liberal links and were demanding a Labour prospective parliamentary candidate for the next election. Only the State was stronger: the National Agricultural Wages Board determined a minimum wage of 25s despite trade union opposition; the Corn Production Act established a price for wheat and oats; the Trade Union (Amalgamated) Act made mergers easier; the Whitley Report on Relations of Employers and Employed suggested wages' councils as a means to settle disputes; the Finance Act raised income tax to 5s in the £; the Excess Profit Duty was now raised to 80% and the War Loan had the power to borrow countless millions. And all these were backed by the continual use of The Defence of the Realm Act. By now the State could keep citizens away from railway tunnels, force them to obtain a permit to use binoculars, deny them a drink of spirits on Saturday and Sunday and forbid them to feed their dog with scraps of food. Only women seemed to be making some progress as nurses, probation officers and even bank-tellers. While the formation of the Scottish Women's Rural Institute (SWRI) in August 1917 and its stress on the traditional values of 'motherhood and housewifery in rural areas' was welcomed, it could not conceal the fact that the female franchise was coming. It was to become law in February 1918.

By the end of 1917 the nation was exhausted, even though only those in high positions knew the true picture of the war costing £7,000,000 a day or £2,550 million a year, and monthly casualty lists running at 56,000. Already fifty-eight former pupils (twenty-three of them officers) from Perth Academy were dead and people were now speaking of a lost generation.

1918

Morale in the city of Perth rose again in 1918. It was common knowledge that the Germans were suffering badly under the Royal Navy's blockade and it was felt that if they could just hang on a little bit more, they would see final victory. Nobody thought it would be easy. Indeed, those with an eye for strategy suspected that there would be at least one more big German push. If only it did not come until the American Army was in France!

Roll Call at Noeux-les-Mines, April 1918

Few would have been so positive had they known that the British Army now had a monthly casualty rate of 75,000. Even with an army of 3,759,000, such a loss could not be sustained for long as the Army was being bled dry. Then there was the cost. How many citizens realised that the war was costing £7,500,000 a day? How many of them, even old soldiers, appreciated the statistics: a division needed 450 tons of supplies a day and the British Army had eighty-eight divisions? How many imagined that as many as 14,000 firms in the UK were involved in munitions' making? Still, the Army was back in the forefront of people's minds.

In Perth it had become obvious to the Army that billeting on the general population had become necessary. Those troops not actually involved in training were encouraged to attend allotments in Jeanfield or to keep fit by constant swimming practice. Soldiers were often needed elsewhere and few of them could be spared for the 1918 harvest. There were other problems: the perpetual search for horse-flesh for ambulance wagons; training troops who were illiterate; and the control of the boisterous Canadian Forestry Corps at Ardittie, near Methven. Then there were the sick. Early in January the problem of discharging men who were mentally ill came to the fore. A Local Government Board circular, dated 4 December 1917, had finally defined 'Neurasthenics' as those prone to 'automatic wandering accompanied by loss of memory' and some of these were placed in the Soldiers' and Sailors' Home in York Place. Other army patients were sent to Friarton Isolation Hospital where, by August, there was even a Cerebro-Spinal Fever Unit. Some ex-soldiers formed the Comrades of the Great War Association to fight for their rights. Sadly, many men like the poet William Soutar (1898-1943), invalided out of the Royal Navy at the age of twenty, were never to lead normal lives.

Recruiting continued remorselessly in the face of ridicule. For instance, a thirty-six year old calender man and a thirty-eight year old foreman cleaner appealed for exemption at the Tribunal and were told that 'they would rather face a dirty carpet than a dirty German!' by Lord Provost Scott, who, a month later, was awarded an OBE. By June the Tribunals were calling up men in the forty-nine to fifty-one age bracket. This caused great difficulty as these men were generally family men.

One such was the last gravedigger for whom the Town Council strove hard to gain exemption. Fortunately, there were female cemetery workers, earning 25s a week. However, the great rush for men came in August by which time the Tribunals had decided that dye-workers could be spared to fight.

This time round it was Frank Eastman who was fighting for key workers in Pullars and he put his argument well. In 1914, he claimed, the Hat Blocking Department had twenty-eight men, now there were only three; the finishers once numbered 240, now there were only eighty; there were once six joiners in Perth, now there were only three, while the six at Tulloch were reduced to one! Almost as bad was the fact that the firm was short of some 300 female staff. Middle-aged men were now being examined for service: a forty-three year old Bristol manager; a fifty year old clerk who bought the firm's dyes and chemicals; a forty-two year old hat blocker who supervised all the machines and a forty-three year old joiner. The office had already lost six, two of whom were dead, one had resigned and three were still serving. Even the Women's Recruiting Rally must have realised that the nation was sweeping the bottom of its barrel. Still, there was a glimmer of hope. October brought the first mention in the press of 'possible demobilisation soon'.

Civilian involvement actually increased in 1918. For example, wastepaper was, for the first time, collected systematically under the National Salvage Council. Children scoured the city, street by street, methodically gathering every piece of scrap metal as well as fruit-stones and hard nutshells which were required for urgent war purposes. Others made clothes for wounded soldiers, collected brambles for jam or gathered herbs. Allotments were everywhere as were flag-sellers and helpers for the YMCA and Salvation Army. Special efforts were made for Perth Tank Week and the Perthshire Voluntary Workers' Association who had announced that Perth's Road-Building Volunteers were now safely in France. More and more War Bonds were purchased and more ground given over to vegetables, while golf courses and recreation grounds were all set aside for 'cropping'.

Aliens were under a closer watch than ever: Moise Abramsky, a Russian; Einar Gunnersen, a Norwegian and 'dangerous persons' like Henry Drucker, Rudolf and Cristian Fehrenbach; Toshio Go, a Japanese and Mary Rosenplaentz whose origin was unknown. The usual problems arose. Was Margaret McRae, now Mrs Hatje, an alien? Who would pay for the Shy family, pork butchers from Northumberland, driven from their home by the mob and lodged in the Queen's Hotel, Perth? What was to be done with US males located in Perth who were trying to dodge military service? With 300,000 German prisoners of war engaged in farm work, some 700 of them working in Perthshire, there was an increasing number of escapes, especially from the Auchterarder Camp. There were three in April, six in May and others in June, August and September.

Inevitably, drink continued to be a major concern and while there was a steady stream of Central Control Board convictions, the police still argued that the courts were not hard enough on offenders. Much of the crime in 1918 was drink-related: drunken women and troops; wife assaults and the occasional rape. The most common offence was bigamy, often committed by deserters. Prostitution and the maintenance of a brothel continued to appear as offences. Then there was the ordinary range of petty crimes of stealing bicycles and reckless cycling with newer offences such as posing as a war hero, working as a card sharp, selling obscene prints and anonymous letter-writing. Butter hoarding seemed on the increase with fifty-two offenders recorded, many of them prominent citizens, as well as graffiti writing and general vandalism.

Having to deal with these offences as well as with normal duties which included local fires and drownings in the river and lake, it is not surprising that the police again wanted a rise. The Chief Constable claimed the Kirkcaldy scale of £275-£350 per annum, the Superintendent £190-£265 per annum, a 10s war bonus for all and one day a week off under the Police Weekly Rest Day (Scotland) Act 1914. The basis for any claim was the vast range of State regulations that the police had to impose. There was the Food Hoarding Order 1917, Butter (Maximum Prices) Order 1917, Milk Order 1918, Meat Retail Prices Order No 2 1918, Rationing Order 1918, Jam (Prices) No 2 Order 1918, Potatoes Order 1918, Sale of Sweetmeats Order 1918, British Onions Order 1918 and many more. They also had to keep up air raid drills and warnings, now made more difficult by the presence of aircraft.

The Town Council, with the same reluctance as in 1914, were still struggling to meet air raid insurance premiums. Pensions too were a monthly drain on the city's limited resources, while the supply of food was a nightmare with its complex State regulations. There were Food Orders, Enforced Orders, National Kitchen Committees, Food Control Committees, and handbooks on National Kitchens. Every month saw some article in short supply. In October for example there was a milk shortage followed by hasty demonstrations on how to get round this. Coal was rationed in Perth from May to October 1918 until the Household Fuel and Lighting (Scotland) Order 1918 and the Price of Coke Order 1918. The Belgians were still a headache with their continual moans for free books for their children and demands for more flag-days, while the tinkers were even worse. A census at the end of October showed that there were 2,728 tinkers. Of these 1,757 were rural and 491 urban; there were 309 in the Army and 171 in industrial schools. The problem, as ever, was how to educate their children. Transport was the key to the city's well being, but by February the tram-workers were asking for 15s above their pre-war rates, while the July-appointed female conductors were demanding a ladies' lavatory plus new uniforms. Given the 8s bonus to junior motormen and the increasing damage caused by vandals, fares had to go up in August. There were other rising costs: in April janitors were awarded 4s and in August teachers demanded the Craik Salary Scale.

In general, trade unions were fairly quiet until June. A few weeks earlier, General Bethune, on behalf of the National Alliance of Employers and Workers, in the Lesser City Hall, had issued a passionate appeal 'that we make a joint effort'. As if to show their power, the trade unions held a huge demonstration on the North Inch on 23 June. But to show that they still had the upper hand, the Town Council refused the Perth Trades and Labour Council the use of the City Hall on Sundays. They may well have done so because of their running battle with the gas workers. Gas was a vital ingredient in the nation's war machine as its by-products included ammonia, benzole, toluol and glycerine which gave the gas workers a great deal of muscle. They had demonstrated this early in January when their strike had plunged the city into darkness and cut off the engines at Pullars and Campbells. It took the presence of a senior official of the Board of Trade to restore peace.

The following month the National Union of General Workers' Conference at York issued a new wage demand: 10s for all workers in gas and electric undertakings and a minimum wage of 21s to all over twenty-one years. Considering that this was strongly backed by James O'Grady MP, who was also Secretary of the National Federation of General Workers, it was likely to succeed. The Town Council gave the assistant gas manager £170 per annum and his bookkeeper £120 per annum. Then the electric workers added a demand for 12½% bonus 'as awarded by the Minister of Munitions on the decision of Sir George Askwith.' They had had 10s over their wage level on 1 January plus the minimum wage of 21s for those over eighteen years and 5s for those who were younger. Women employed on men's work were given the same advance. They even managed to win double time for Sundays. Next came their 12% bonus which was paid out in April. However, they were not finished yet. Late in April a further award of 4s was made for those whose advances were under 4s weekly. With the gas treasurer earning the huge sum of £300 per annum, there were other rises. Gas collectors received 6s bonus in May and foremen 4s in June. By September the Town Council had had enough. No more cash would be available. Nevertheless, when the Electrical Power Engineers' Association complained that some of their members were still not receiving their rise above the pre-war rates nor the 12½% bonus, these were granted immediately. Incredibly, as the result of another demand for arbitration they were granted a further 3s 6d in October.

The corporation workers had watched the success of the gas and electric men with amazement. They then demanded arbitration as well under Sir James Urquhart and their wage case covering sweepers, firemen, lighting workers, power and paving men was sent to the Committee on Production. The arbitration was held in Glasgow and the award, 7s for men and 4s 6d for women, was backdated to 12 December 1917. The Town Council tried to explain that wages were already high. After all, two female clerks earned 25s each as did two female slot-meter collectors and even a boy slot-meter collector had 20s. A whole string of rises followed despite opposition from the Town Council. Baths foremen were awarded 6s 6d and female attendants, 4s 6d, burial workers, 4s and cleansing firemen, 4s. The Isolation staff matron received £10, the sister, £5 and the cook and maids £5 each. The City Hall keeper was given 5s, the Town Clerk's typists, 3s, cleaners, 2s, the Registrar's assistant 2s 6d and a war bonus of 3s. With the superintendent of the Canal Street washhouse earning 60s a week, the two burgh surveyors asked for higher war bonuses but were told that they had already received 2s on 6 November 1916 and 2s in January 1917. Although the town officer was given 6s 6d, it was the June demand from the watermen for a 12½% bonus that really alarmed the Town Council. They were only given 5s. Three months later, thanks to the National Union of General Workers, they received a further 4s and a 12½% bonus. As the year drew to a close, all the corporation workers were told by the Town Council to arbitrate or strike when they asked for 25s above their pre-war rates.

Carters, led by the renowned Hugh Lyon, gave the Town Council a problem when they refused a 6s rise and asked for arbitration. Sir James Urquhart awarded 7s to the slaughter-men and the road roller-men. Then, in February, the Town Council and the Co-op Society allied to fight a Motormen's Association claim for the carters: 20s on pre-war rates and time and a half for overtime. They were given the former, but not the latter. The Co-op carters were not pleased and went on strike demanding 25s over the pre-war rate which was allowed in most burghs. Firemen too provided an embarrassing situation. The Secretary of the National Union of General Workers claimed that Perth's fire-master had threatened to clear out all the union members as soon as he could. He was given leave of absence while the Town Council investigated the matter. Three months later the firemen were also given 20s over pre-war rates and a 12½% bonus. The city's tradesmen were keen to enter this race for wages and in April they did so. The joiners were the first, demanding 2d more an hour which was granted. The printers were next and their rise took them to 50s a week, while the tailors asked in vain and the bakers were given 17s so as not to strike.

As for the big firms in Perth, it was significant that the North British Dyeworks did not publish its customary start-of-the-year report. Some workers had already left Pullars convinced that it now had no future. The Dyers' Union, on the other hand, felt strong. At a January rally in the City Hall, attended by 600, the local branch president, James Taylor, launched a savage attack on non-union workers. The meeting endorsed his view by voting for a closed-shop policy with an increasing penalty for those who delayed in joining. The city paid little attention to this demand, being more interested in the possibility that the city might profit from captured German dye secrets.

Then, on 6 March, the *Perthshire Advertiser* declared: 'Hint of definite change coming!' and that Messrs Eastman and Sons Limited, London 'were interested in Pullars.' A week later the city found out that Eastmans had acquired 'a controlling interest' and that 'the Pullar family no longer have responsibility.' A wave of relief swept the community. There would be no closure and the famous Pullars' name would be retained.

Meanwhile, the Dyers' Union had held a wage meeting in the City Hall which attracted 1,300. On this occasion the most vocal were the male dyers who demanded 20s over the pre-war rates. This irritated the women in the Ironing Department and a noisy debate followed. Finally, it was resolved that all females in the North British Dye Works over eighteen years of age should have at least 25s a week. Naturally alarmed by this fresh demand, A E Pullar asked the workers to send him a delegation with proposals. While these discussions were underway, the union revived its crusade against non-unionists, arguing that they were not entitled to the latest rise. They warned that they only had seven days left to enlist in the union. A E Pullar was furious: 'We will not distinguish between unionists and non-unionists … and the British people are free people and the workers are entitled to decide in regard to their membership with trade unions.' That night the factory walls were disfigured by graffiti.

On 8 April, the *Constitutional* announced that the firm was under new management: Eastman and Sons. The editor, on behalf of Pullars, was careful to explain that this was not an amalgamation, but 'simply providing new management.' The Pullar family added their own explanation: 'We have to inform you that Messrs Eastman and Sons, Dyers and Cleaners, Limited, Acton Vale, London, have acquired a controlling interest in this business as from 31 December, 1917 … the Pullar family will retain an interest, but will not have any responsibility in the management.' Almost at once the Royal Warrant was granted to Eastmans and the latter decided to employ Campbells' workers as well. On 5 June, the *Constitutional* revealed the arbiter's pay award on the Dyers' Union *vs* John Pullar and Sons Limited dispute. For those over thirty-one years, the following awards were made: skilled male dyers, 5s; skilled dry cleaners, wet cleaners and finishers, 4s; and labourers, 3s. Men aged 25-30 would receive 'part rises' and women on time-rates and over eighteen years (except clerks and typists) would receive 3s. 'Merit advances' would be over and above these awards and would include overtime rates. The rises would start on 15 April and they would be reconsidered in six months from 15 May with a month's notice either side. They would not be paid in slack months except by agreement after six months. These arrangements were for abnormal conditions due to the war.

The new management at Pullars announced the setting up of a Works' Council where questions affecting Works conditions and employment could be brought up for consideration by elected representatives of the workers, and conferences could be arranged between the Council and the directors when necessary. Workers' representatives would be elected annually in two sections, Perth and Tulloch. The first meeting, with William Eastman in the chair, took place on 7 October. The *Perthshire Advertiser* on 9 October described this as 'an interesting innovation' from the Whitley Report. Managers, foremen, forewomen, those under eighteen years of age and those employed there for less than six months were not allowed to vote. Workers' nominees were expected to be by department and they could elect their own chairman and secretary. Co-opted members were allowed, two from Perth and one from Tulloch. Although there was, as yet, no constitution, according to the *Perth Courier*, 'the Council was in no way antagonistic to trade unionism ... admitting the rights of workers' combinations and accepting it as being in accordance with the trends of modern industrial life ... the workers being as much interested in the prosperity of the business as were the directors ... it was for discussion and advice rather than administration and they would cover works regulations, meal hours, comfort, health and suggested improvements.' Both sides agreed that the future was assured if there was co-operation and mutual confidence.

Meanwhile P and P Campbell had endured great difficulties, but as 1918 neared its close there were more dyes available and the full fifty-one hour week was restored. Although wages were paid in the slack season, holidays honoured, minimum wages guaranteed for piece workers, and discharged soldiers employed, there had been no new plant installed for years. Thomson's Fair City Dyeworks had struggled all year to keep dyeing in the list of 'certified occupations' while fighting for exemptions for its few remaining skilled men. Garvie and Deas Dyeworks had to fight to challenge their workers' claim for an extra 10s against J C Hendry, Organiser of the Textile Union. Coates' Balhousie Works had huge government contracts in March when they had been forced to fall back on a forty-hour week which was then followed by a sex scandal involving Henry Coates. Steam laundries had generally done well and Perth Steam Laundry, Dunkeld Road, had no problem in giving its workers a rise of 5%.

Shields' Wallace Works was less fortunate. Having announced a profit of £18,917, two of their managers died suddenly, and the Perth Textile Workers' Union demanded a rise. The firm's offer of 4s to men, 3s to women over eighteen and 2s to those under eighteen, was rejected. The union demanded 7s for men over twenty-one years, 4s for those between eighteen and twenty-one and 2s for women under eighteen years. These figures, the union claimed, were based on statistics from the Committee on Production. They also demanded 20s on pre-war rates and a 12½% war bonus with the threat that they would hand in their notices on 28 August. On Saturday, 17 August, H G Shields, the managing director, offered 1s to 5s, but J Hendry of the Textile Unions turned the offer down. The union wanted their bonuses plus arrears. As promised they closed the Works on 28 August without any demonstration by workers, held a ballot and found that only six wanted to accept the management's offer while 262 rejected it. Some 1,000 were affected by this shutdown. The workers refused to hear the views of the Chief Industrial Commissioners, they collected their *lying-money* and sent Hendry off to London. The Government knew that the strikers were adamant; they had already proved that in their previous strike in July. On

8 October, the arbiter appointed by the Minister of Labour, Professor J M Irvine KC, gave the full award from 15 July. This amounted to more than the firm had offered by 2s for men over twenty-one years and 1s for women over eighteen years. The firm, however, had the last word: there had been a lack of skilled men, too many government regulations and the cost of materials was still too high.

The effect of all these rises was that by 1918 wages were, in general, roughly twice those of 1914. But prices were far higher. If the July 1914 price index is taken to have been 100, then by July 1918 it was 218 and by November 1918 it was 233. In other words, prices were rising faster than ever as the war drew to its end. A 1914 blouse, for instance, once 1s 3½d was now 6s 11d. Clothing had never been scarce, just expensive.

The Government was anxious to hide the real situation in Britain, the food queues especially, under a mass of Ministry of Food statistics and films like *The Folk Back Home* and slogans, such as, 'Smile Across the Channel!' A food bill which in 1914 would have cost 20s was now 47s 3d because eggs were 3s 6d a dozen and a rabbit 4s 9d, while beef at 1s 10d, steak at 2s 2d, mutton at 1s 10d and chops at 1s 8d were beyond the means of many. Although the price of wheat, at 72s 10d a quarter, was falling, the prices for food paid by the Perth School Board in 1915 had risen as follows by 1918: potatoes 2s 9d to 7s; turnips 3s to 6s 8d; carrots 7s to 24s; whole rice 24s to 33s; ground rice 16s to 37s 4d; sugar 32s to 56s; barley 2s 9d to 4s 6d; lentils 25s to 61s; flour 22s to 26s. Perth had one meatless day a week in January and it laid on many samples of food economy for women. In February, the city, like many others, started a meat-rationing scheme. But such informal rationing schemes did not work well despite a huge rise in rates to 2s 4d in the £ to give the city some capital. Formal rationing of meat, lard, bacon and margarine began in Perth on 14 July 1918. Soon, this had to be extended to sugar, butter, jam, tea and cheese. Although supplies of meat were adequate by the summer, the price in Perth still rose by 2d per lb in August, and coal and coke rose by another 1s 6d a ton. Meanwhile the Government made sure that the public knew that prices were far higher in Germany where eggs cost 1s each and a cabbage 12s. If people had known that over 760,000 German civilians were to die in the Royal Navy blockade of Germany they would have been horrified.

The cinema had suffered a heavy blow with the Entertainment Tax of 1916, but was anxious to recoup its losses through higher prices and more attractive use of colour and animation. In Perth, safety measures were improved, while licences continued to change hands. Propaganda was used with greater skill as the end of the war approached to show that child welfare was close to the Government's heart and that with the Maternity and Child Welfare Act 1918 there would be home help schemes and clinics everywhere.

Many began to argue for the creation of a Ministry of Health and greater participation by the State. There seemed good justification for this view in Perth as 'The Spanish Flu' laid low 1,293 children and sixteen teachers in September. Other factors contributed as well. There were questions of whether illegitimacy was increasing and how to care for the many unmarried mothers. Although there was more venereal disease in the city, there was now a bacteriologist to deal with it. There were even fewer blind and fewer elderly poor, while marriages were once again on the increase.

The State seemed stronger than ever and the phrase 'State collectivism' was often heard. Its power was exemplified by the fact that it now taxed eight million people compared to just over a million in 1914. Not that socialist views were strong in Perth. The Town Council rejected the idea of land nationalization and was not too keen on the opening of Labour Rooms in Methven Street. Women, however, were continuing to make progress. The Scottish Women's Rural Institute had spread to Braco and Greenloaning in April, and to Meigle and Pitlochry by October. All the junior students at Perth Academy training to be teachers were female and women were safely ensconced in Perth's Probation Service. In April the Town Council debated the Representation of the People Act 1918 which most believed had come about as a result of the war.

Then with almost a brutal suddenness, news reached Perth at 11 a.m on 11 November 1918 that the war was over. The bells rang out from the tower of St John's Kirk, flags were hoisted and an evening service was held in the City Hall.

1918-1922

When news of the ceasefire reached Perth on 11 November 1918, the whole community was swept by a wave of gratitude and relief. It did not last long. The reason was simple: the people were exhausted and there was no place for jubilation, no matter what hysterical Londoners may have thought. This was in vivid contrast to Mafeking Night on 21 May 1900 when the entire city had gone mad with joy. Indeed, there was even a feeling of disbelief that an ordeal such as the war could at last be over. The authorities sensed the mood and declared a public holiday on 13 November. Nevertheless, it took a long time to arrange Peace Day celebrations. They were eventually scheduled for Saturday, 19 July 1920 and to make sure that participants remained sober, the Central Control Board decreed that all licensed grocers would close for the day and pubs would only open from 4 p.m-6.30 p.m.

Serving soldiers, however, just wanted home and out of uniform as soon as possible. Although it had long been suspected that there would be problems in disbanding such a large body of men, attempts to work out some kind of priority system were swamped by the rush. Perth was witness to an early example of 'demob blues'. On 18 November, one of the first groups of nine local men who had all previously worked for the Town Council's Roads and Streets Department was discharged from the City Hall. Now they wanted their jobs back. A worried burgh surveyor told the Town Council: 'We can't take nine back! It will add £400 to a £1,300 wage bill. Anyway, there is no work for so many. We would have to sack five or six of the present force and don't forget the pension problem!' Fortunately, three of the temporary holders of positions were over seventy years old. Nonetheless, this incident shows the root of the problem: the men wanted back as soon as they could before their jobs disappeared. Others felt the same, especially the 10,000 held in camp at Folkestone who rioted on 3 January 1919. In February, another 3,000 rioted in London and others in Glasgow, Epsom and Coventry. In March, lives were lost when the Canadians rioted in North Wales and in July, Luton Town Hall was burned down. The military did the best they could. By 8 January 1919, 300,000 had been released and thereafter 4,000 were released daily. Many blamed Lloyd George's eagerness to get voters for the rush but that did not stop other disturbances at Wolverhampton, Salisbury and Swindon. By August, 2,732,105 men had been demobbed. Nevertheless this did not deter families from pleading for an early release of their loved ones on compassionate grounds. Scotland shared the unrest: the Black Watch refused to board a ship which they suspected would take them to fight in Russia. There was a similar refusal from one hundred Highland Light Infantry in Edinburgh, two hundred Scottish Rifles at Leith, the 459th Agricultural Company at Stirling, seven hundred Seaforths at Cromarty and minesweeper crews at Rosyth.

While most of the 5,500,000 men who had served in France were probably left with no illusions about the effects of war, that was not the case with many civilians who seemed to think that the war had brought changes which would lead to a better world. In Perth, there was a clear conviction that the future would be happier, certainly for the young. After all, education was to be compulsory to the age of fourteen and this was to be followed by day-continuation classes. Primary fees, part-timers, early-leavers would all be things of the past. There was even a strong belief that normality was just around the corner. The General Accident Insurance Company made a rapid recovery as motorcar insurance took off. Their income, which was £1,709.000 in 1917, soared to £3,315,000 in 1920 and £4,965,000 in 1923. Business euphoria appeared to sweep Scotland.

Unwinding, however, proved to be a slow and lengthy process. Within a week the National Kitchen Scheme was abandoned, the Aliens' Restrictions Orders relaxed and all General Orders for the Police cancelled. Then it was announced that 'our alien friends' had no need to report to the authorities regularly. Prisoners of war were different. They still tried to escape and many stole what they could. Pigeons were freed and Lighting Regulations for Shop Windows were lifted. The War Office even asked the Town Council if they would like any war relics. In

January 1919, work began on the rebuilding of the harbour railway and some war charities were closed down. Flag-days for discharged soldiers and sailors were allowed to continue. Then, to the great joy of all, the Belgian refugees left Perth in small groups. By October they were all away and R M Pullar formally thanked the Town Council for the use of the City Chambers and the rate-free accommodation for the Belgians. Jeanfield residents asked that the balance of their Comforts Fund go towards a Memorial Fountain in the park, while the Town Council proposed that the city's restoration of St John's Kirk be its contribution. Sadly, they were to find that a compilation of a Roll of Honour was no easy task.

In March, boat-hiring began again on the Tay and the North Inch golf course was restored. Plans were made for the traditional Perthshire Agricultural Show on the South Inch and the laying of underground telegraph lines recommenced. April saw the first civilian flag day - the Children's League of Pity - and, while advertisements reappeared in railway stations, the city's councillors returned from war. As treats were laid on for children of deceased soldiers, German and Austrian ex-prisoners of war marched to the general station for their journey home. Early in June, the Army finally left the Poorhouse, selling off surplus supplies, while the Red Cross quitted the Old Infirmary in York Place. Just as peace was formally announced, the Pullar family presented the Perth and Perthshire Memorial Fund with a splendid donation of £1,000.

The unwinding process speeded up in 1920 with the abolition of conscription and the Liquor Control Board. Resentment towards conscientious objectors began to fade and even war relics lost their popularity. Some services, however, were still inadequate. There were postal delays to the US due to conditions not yet returning to normal and a lack of fast steamers. Then, as the year ended, the Army Pay Corps evacuated the corner of Atholl Street/Kinnoull Street and Pullars quickly moved in to convert the building into workers' flats. Craigie Knowes allotments were closed while the continuation of the Jeanfield allotments reflected local interest.

Even though Perth had no fewer than a tank and six guns to place around the city, the manager of King James V1 Hospital refused all of them. By 1920, the Town Council also had no great enthusiasm for more memorials and refused to donate cash to the Zeebrugge Memorial; it went, instead, to paint seats around the North Inch. Unbelievably, it was not until the summer of 1922 that the Town Council knew what to do with its war souvenirs. Having sold the tank's engine to a firm in Motherwell, the tank went to Craigie Knowes and the Turkish guns to the Barracks. There was nearly as much trouble with the city's Roll of Honour, particularly for the county. If a man had been born in one parish, but had lived in another, which could claim him? It was far easier to ban the grazing of cows on the North Inch.

The return of the Black Watch battalions made many people ponder on what the war had cost. It was obvious that many of the returning soldiers were restless and found it hard to settle. Some offered their skills to the Royal Irish Constabulary and even more to the Black and Tans. By July 1920, the Territorial Army had revived and was soon advocating the formation of a Defence Force. The Royal Air Force began actively seeking recruits in the Perth area by August, while Black Watch recruiting started again in May 1921. There was no loss of enthusiasm for service with the colours, rather the reverse, as young men listened in awe to the stirring tales of their elders in the Ex-Servicemen's Club or the various Territorial Army Associations. Much of it was sheer romance, because it was generally accepted that there would be no major war for the next ten years at least. In Perth, the Town Council and the military began to irritate each other once again. The former refused the Army a military sports ground near the Barracks and the latter responded by turning their canteen into a retail unit.

It took years for estimates of casualties to be collated. For schools it was relatively easy: Perth Academy lost two teachers and 165 pupils; Glenalmond, seven teachers and 157 pupils; Morrison's Academy, one teacher and seventy-two pupils; Ardvreck, sixty-four pupils. Herein lay the seeds of the 'Lost Generation Theory' of later years. Businesses were in a parallel situation: Pullars lost sixty-one and the General Accident Insurance Company thirty-eight. As for Scotland as a whole, 573,000 served and 116,000 died, Glasgow alone losing 18,000 or 10% of its adult males. Perth had been equally patriotic. Out of 10,121 men of military age, 3,997 had served and about a thousand, some 25% of those who served or 10% of the adult males, had perished. In the county, out of 35,199 men on the rolls, 11,357 had served, 32.6% of those available. Sadly, the dead were aged between twenty and forty years, mainly young infantrymen, although many were middle-class officers.

At the personal level, one family's story was typical. Tom Pearson, a mason earning 50s a week, lived with his wife and a daughter who made 24s a week. He had ten sons: Sergeant David, 11th Royal Scots, lost two legs and had a pension of 32s 6d a week; Private Robert, 10th Scottish Rifles, was killed in action; Private John, 10th Black Watch was working. Still serving were: Sergeant Tom, 3rd Seaforths; Private William, Army Service Corps; Private James, Royal Flying Corps; Private Joseph, 3rd Scottish Rifles; Private Charles, 1st/6th Black Watch; and Private Alex, 52nd Graduating Battalion, Gordon Highlanders. Private George, 14th Black Watch, was working. Mrs Pearson who received 6s 9d wrote to the Army asking that the youngest, Alex, be released to carry his crippled brother to their tenement toilet.

The United Kingdom was left with 190,000 widow pensioners and 10,000 orphan pensioners. The human suffering was immense. In 1919, Perth had two blind soldiers, five permanent cases in the Asylum and 253 seriously wounded in Perth Royal Infirmary. Of these, even as late as 1922, there were still forty-five receiving daily treatment. Roaming the countryside to the annoyance of the police were dozens of mentally crippled ex-soldiers. The cost of the war in sterling was enormous, equivalent to at least eight years' peaceful wealth and was continuous, although diminishing. In 1919, it was £692m, in 1920, £292m and in 1921, £189m.

The Town Council were particularly devoted to the idea of normality and to them the period 1918-1922 was essentially a reconstruction era. Although prices were still rising in Perth, there was a feeling of speculative boom as wartime profits were spent. It was felt that pre-war conditions would return and with them a demand for British goods, hence the wish to return to the Gold Standard. The people of Perth were full of hope as they looked at the city's prospects and had many plans: to turn Kinnoull Hill into a recreation park; to eliminate smoke pollution; to develop hydro-electric power; to control annual flooding; to bring in new industry and to develop radio communication.

But none of it was to be. The city was continually short of power between 1919 and 1921 and there were periods of fuel economy, coal emergency and short supply. There were times when there was so little coal that gas could not be made, or when gas pressure had to be reduced to save coal, or when the price of coal soared by 6s a ton. There were still problems over food supply and difficulties working with the Food Control Committee, the Profiteering Committee and the Perth Allotment and Garden Food Association. Even as late as 1921, allotments were considered vital for the city's food requirements. There was also a shortage of money. In 1919 the city asked the Government for cash and tried to acquire a Victory War Loan. Even a Falkirk proposal for a National Bank which would give local authorities interest-free loans was considered, but when this fell through, an economy drive was introduced by taking away officials' home telephones. The War Pension Acts of 1915-1920 were an especial headache even though eleven members of the Town Council were on the Pensions' Committee.

One particularly embarrassing effect of the war was the rundown of fire equipment which the Town Council were unable to replace due to lack of money. If they had hoped for a conflagration-free period they were disappointed. A Hillyland fire in January led to the exposure to the press of pipes full of holes. But the purchase of a new tractor for the fire engine and a dispute over tied houses delayed any new equipment. Disaster struck with a £250,000 fire at P and P Campbell's Perth Dye Works in May 1919 which was detailed in the *Perthshire Advertiser* under the heading: 'Severe Criticism of Brigade.' The insurance investigator's report read: 'The equipment was most primitive and ineffective, a disgrace to a city the size of Perth ... the fire engine was wretched and a comic apology.' To the horror of the local Rotary Club there was a threat not to insure any business in Perth. The Town Council promised to improve their equipment, but before they could do so there was an even more disastrous fire at Messrs A Bell and Sons, Horner's Lane. The loss in whisky was estimated at £300,000 and a hundred people lost their homes. The Town Council had no option: they bought a new fire engine at once. Four months later they even had a new Fire Station in King Edward Street, thanks to the generosity of Miss Rachael Pennycook of Craigie, who consequently earned herself the freedom of the city. This enabled the city to buy two fire engines. Meanwhile, firemen, realising how important they were, demanded a weekly wage of 70s and later a scale to 90s. There were other fires in 1922: a £12,000 blaze at the BB Cinema in January, and a £10,000 fire at McEwan's store in May. A sign of modernisation was the replacement of the old brass headgear of the firemen with leather helmets.

As for the police, they were convinced within months that normality had returned, at least as far as crime was concerned. *Shebeening*, poaching, thieving, stone-throwing, vandalism, children street-begging, graffiti writing and reckless driving were all back again, as before. Specific war crimes such as passing dud cheques, wearing uniform and decorations illegally and desertion were dwindling. Bigamy, which had flourished with the end of the war, was the exception. And there were fairly new offences: photo-conmen and bogus war charity collectors. But most alarming, however, was the fact that society was awash with guns. Police feared that these weapons would end up in the hands of Sinn Féin and the fear was justified when a notorious Sinn Féiner from Valleyfield in Fife stole four revolvers from the Barracks. Sinn Féin was certainly active in Perth and several of their members ended up in Perth Penitentiary. The police judgement on crime was ominous: 'Prison is no longer a deterrent against evil doing.' This seemed obvious with a return to an increase in vagrants, many of whom were deserters living off thieving.

Many of the police welcomed the return to whipping juvenile offenders and were dismayed by their inability to control the noisy crowds of dancers who rolled home at two or three o'clock in the morning. Another disappointment had been the failure of the poll in December 1920 under the Temperance (Scotland) Act 1913 and No 21 Temperance (Scotland) Act Regulations 1920 in six Perth wards. Only 67% of voters had taken the trouble to participate and of these the majority saw no reason for any change. In October 1921 the United Free Churches in Perth renewed their campaign against the drink trade, but were outmanoeuvred by the Licensed Trade Defence Association with the result that opening times now were 11.30 a.m to 2.30 p.m and 4.30

p.m to 9.30 p.m. The fact that drink interests were too strong was proved by the April 1924 re-run of the poll of 1920 which produced the same result. In fact, Perth was still viewed as 'drunken Perth' in 1923 when it was estimated that some £250,000 per annum was spent on drink! However, some claimed that Saturday night 'wife-beating' had declined. Human sexuality did not appear to have changed and although there were more divorces, there was just as much prostitution as before.

In the light of the above, the police felt they were justified in asking for substantial rises which they were granted. In November 1918, a Perth police constable was on a scale of 27s 5d to 36s 9d and a sergeant 37s 11d to 43s 9d. Within a year these scales were 70s to 95s and 100s to 112s 6d, clearly inspired by the police strike of 1919, during which there was a rise in crime. The police force was now a good career choice as the perks of boot and rent allowances, as well as overtime rates, had all increased. Senior officers' salaries had risen substantially at the same time. Women police constables 'of considerable value in certain aspects' were under consideration and electric lamps had now replaced the old oil lamps in their buildings.

One area presenting the Town Council with an air of urgency was housing. The Council knew that the city required at least two hundred new houses immediately and in March 1919 they set up meetings with factors and architects to determine what kind of houses were needed. They were certainly under pressure. A deputation of the city's leading citizens and clerics, Smythe, Shillinglaw and Landreth, declared that the lack of new housing was an emergency and that far more than two hundred were needed.

The Town Council listed all those houses considered 'unlet' and 'condemned' and decided that four hundred were required. Consequently they planned sites in Scone and Dunkeld Road and Darnhall Drive. But before they could negotiate further, a housing demonstration in the City Hall demanding three hundred houses at once forced their hand. Not long after work had started at these sites, the Town Planning (Scotland) Act 1919 became law. Clearly an emergency measure, it compelled local authorities to provide housing to a standard design and guaranteed subsidies. It also made them conduct a speedy survey of housing needs and report proposals to the Health Ministry 'there being a state subsidy for all the costs of council-house building that can't be met by a 1d in £ rate increase.' Other legislation soon followed: the Increase of Rent and Mortgage Interest (War Restrictions) Act 1919 which continued controls and restricted rent increases to a maximum of 10% and the Housing (Additional Powers) Act 1919 which offered subsidies for houses built by private enterprise. By 1920 therefore, housing was a very important topic for the Town Council for whom there was plenty of previous legislation such as the Housing and Town Planning Acts 1890-1908 and the Letting and Rating Act 1913.

The Legislation did little to solve some problems. While there were houses considered unfit in Thimblerow, what was to be done with the tenants? Then there was the matter of building costs: 1,000 bricks had risen in price from 36s to 81s 6d and 1,000 slates from £11 13s 0d to £27 10s 0d. Some houses were positively dangerous: Clayholes; 158 High Street; and 48 George Street, while upgrading the sewers would be really expensive. Conferences were held and data exchanged. Finally, in April 1920, some twenty-eight different areas were identified where houses even lacked water-closets. In ten areas alone, there were forty-one sub-standard houses. There were ten in West Mill Street, seven in Meal Vennel, four in Leonard Street, three in South Street, three in Murray Street, two in Pomarium, two in Bridge Lane, two in Cutlog Vennel and one in Horner's Lane. But there were many questions. What rent would be charged for new houses? How would new houses be allocated? Would the Scottish Veterans' Association be given priority? How would tinkers be housed?

Some answers soon emerged. The Town Council would borrow £60,000 and build sixteen new houses in Darnhall Drive and forty in Dunkeld Road. Rents would be £24 per annum for three apartments and £28 per annum for four. Tinkers would be housed (temporarily) in army huts. Instantly, eight landlords appealed: Mrs Pilkington, who owned seven houses in Keir Street, claimed she had no money owing to the Rent Restriction Act and thus no return on her property for six years; Mrs Murray, who owned the three houses in Murray Street, claimed that she had had no rent increase in thirty years and Mrs Low, who owned four houses in Leonard Street, said she had no funds. The Town Council responded by placing closing orders on some of them and selected another thirteen for immediate conversion: four in Whitefriars; three in Commercial Street; two in High Street, one in Pomarium; one in Craigie Place; one in South William Street; and one in St Catherine's Road - thirteen in all. By 1920, however, the end of 'enhanced purchasing power' had come and by 1922, the Geddes Axe put a stop to new house building. Despite trying hard to live up to modern ideas of designed towns, rationalised land use and restricted urban sprawl, high costs defeated the Town Council.

Another area in which costs were rising was health. Electric treatment, X-rays, massage and the appointment of bacteriologists and radiologists meant that health could only improve with money spent. Fortunately, the establishment of the Ministry of Health and the Scottish Board of Health in 1919 brought about revolutionary changes in public administration. Much legislation flowed from these changes: the Nurses Registration (Scotland) Act and the Blind Persons Act for instance. The decision to pasteurise milk was taken in 1922.

More thought was now given to current problems and statistical analysis and while illegitimacy and its causes were still a mystery, at least there was agreement that war conditions had had no serious effect on health. Alcoholism was increasing, even though malnutrition was dwindling. Tuberculosis was now the challenge that smallpox and typhus had been in the past. Perth appointed a TB officer whose TB scheme was soon in operation. Army huts would be used until a hundred-bed sanatorium was prepared and there would be constant updating of research. Two problems presented themselves: discharged TB soldiers and TB emigrants to the colonies. Much was done to assist both groups. Concern about venereal disease had continued after the war and the appointment of a VD officer and the preparation of a VD scheme with six beds were only the first steps in an attack on the illness. Fortunately, local authorities were obliged to give free diagnosis and treatment and by 1924, Perth Royal Infirmary was treating seventy patients. Disease, of course, comes in waves: typhoid in 1919 and smallpox in 1920, with their accompanying rush for vaccines. Health weeks and cleaning stations for verminous children were both important aids in fighting disease.

The happiest and most successful area of health concerned infants. Between 1916 and 1922, infant mortality in the UK fell by 30%, in large measure due to the Maternity Services and Child Welfare Scheme which required home visits. In March 1919, no fewer than 113 mothers visited the Perth Child Clinic and these increased to 136 by May 1919 and to the astonishing figure of 318 in April 1920. Much of the credit was due to the appointment in June 1919 of a child welfare officer and another health visitor, combined with a greater concern for infant nutrition.

One aspect that left the Town Council completely out of their depth was the new trend in unemployment. Heretofore, the unemployed had generally been the shiftless or unskilled with the occasional, short, irregular lay-offs for the skilled, but now it was the latter who were unemployed long-term. The difficulty for the Council began in April 1920 when the Ministry of Labour wanted to find out the numbers of unemployed ex-soldiers in Perth and the county. To their horror the Town Council found 119 traditionally unskilled looking for work, but also 572 ex-soldiers, fifty-four of whom were disabled. They speedily urged the employment of the disabled and applied to the National Relief Fund for £500. Still the numbers grew and the Town Council tried desperately hard to understand the situation and to devise a solution. They opened their own Unemployed Relief Fund for 651, allowed those with nowhere to go to use the City Hall, hired others to clear the snow off the streets, encouraged the thirty-six 'Dundee Unemployed Marchers to London', tried to help a Co-op St Cuthbert-style laundry for bag-wash organised by out-of-work Perth Dyers and did what they could to combat the demoralising effect of unemployment. Even the State seemed ineffectual despite the Unemployment Insurance Act 1920 and the introduction of the dole, 'uncovenanted benefits.' In January 1922, the Unemployment Grants Committee which paid 60% of the money to the unemployed, reported to the Town Council that its money was exhausted.

Although the average out-of-work man only received 15s plus 5s for his wife and a 1s per child, dole costs soared as unemployment never fell below 9% and the National Unemployed Workers' Movement was founded. While some described the crisis as 'purely regional', the numbers grew and by April 1922 in Perth, it was estimated that there were 824 long-term and 709 short-term unemployed, a total of 1,533. The situation improved over the summer of 1922: 790 in April; 775 in May; 663 in June and 564 in July, but worsened in December 1922 when the figure rose to 816. Little was it known that much worse lay ahead.

One pre-war mystery at least had been resolved and that was poverty. Now it was generally agreed that it was a wage problem and that was the reason that the war had reduced pauperism to a very low ebb. Consequently, 'the undeserving poor' belief began to dissolve and there was a greater degree of sensitivity by the authorities. For example, the term 'Poorhouse' was removed from birth certificates and Perth Poorhouse was renamed Bertha Home in 1922. The more perceptive in society realised that it was not State intervention which had improved the position of so many, but simply higher earnings.

Unemployment tended to reverse the advantages of higher earnings in 1920. Unfortunately, the end of price controls also inflicted damage as prices rose all over the UK. Eggs were often 9d each, bread rose from 9½d to 1s 1d in 1920 and 1s 2½d in 1921, while gas increased by 10d per 1,000 cubic feet due to the coal strike. Poverty returned with a vengeance and in December 1922 some 459 applied for admission to the Poorhouse. Indeed, in 1920 it was reckoned that prices were triple those of 1914 and the situation was worse than in 1918. Many felt that one of the causes was the fact that wages were too high and differentials too low. In 1920, a mason had 97s 2d while his labourer had 84s, a rail porter had 72s 11d and a painter 96s 3d. The end of the Profiteering Act 1919 in May 1921 and rationing in November 1922 helped to ease matters. The price of wheat steadily fell thereafter: 80s 10d a quarter in 1920; 71s 6d in 1921 and 47s 10d in 1922.

Few city employees in the Transport Department would have believed a word of the above. They pushed hard for continuous rises until, by 1920, a driver had 70s a week. Then their trade union, the National Transport Workers' Federation, submitted a claim for 44s over pre-war rates and threatened, if rejected, to strike on 3 April 1920. The Town Council described the demand as 'excessive' and the *Constitutional* as 'colossal'. The union, realising it had over-reached itself, backed down, but two months later it was back with a general wage demand. The Town Council gave them 5s and put up bus fares. Unbelievably, they returned four months later asking for another 12s, but this was spurned.

Labour Exchange, King Edward Street

Photograph courtesy of Perth Museum & Art Gallery, Perth & Kinross Council, Scotland

The Town Council had to be careful in handling transport difficulties as transport was central to their revenue. There were many problems: female workers pushing for equal pay; ex-soldiers with poor health being sued by private bus companies and tram and bus accidents. They also had the costly responsibility of extending bus services and acquiring more trams. By 1920, it was obvious that more capital should go to buses and a Commer and a Strakers Squire were bought. The Council then had to economise by dyeing discarded army uniforms for their staff and cutting back in wages by 3s in February 1921 and 4s in November 1922.

But it was with the other municipal employees that the Town Council found out the headaches that went with union negotiations. In February 1920, the Amalgamated Society of Engineers demanded that their bonus be merged with their wage to give them an extra 3s 4½d, while the Association of Blacksmiths and the Ironworkers' Society won their members a wage rise from 83s 4½d to 86s 9d in six months. Then the Amalgamated Society of Carpenters objected to their members being used for rough work out of doors as the National Union of Clerks demanded a new scale of 70s for workers at the age of twenty-one. The National Association of Technical Gas Officials complained about their members' low salaries and suggested £847 per annum for an engineer, just as the Scottish Association of Paviors' Federation won their members an extra 3d an hour. In November 1920, the United Operative Associates of Scotland deplored the use of unskilled labour to do their members' work. The most powerful was the National Union of General Workers, which, in February 1919, argued for 30s over pre-war rates and a forty-four hour week. After a long, protracted struggle they gained 30s and a forty-seven hour week. Their general aim was an overall 60s weekly and this they achieved for cleansing and lighting staff by July 1920. They even managed a spectacular 7s for electricity workers and a new scale for technical staff. These forced the councillors to face a never-ending wave of pressure: deputations threatening to strike; demands for war bonuses; claims for huge rises; applications for double time; arguments for a minimum wage and shorter hours; higher shift rates; and holidays with pay.

The Town Council did the best they could. They refused to replace men who retired, they cut back on staff numbers, others they sacked, some rises they rejected and others they ignored. The problems must have seemed never-ending: satisfying disabled men asking for lighter work; changing schedules to absorb men who had been promised their jobs back; rejecting legal claims for compensation; buying a new five-ton Commer lorry for the gas works at £1,170 and a new tipping vehicle for cleansing. Their strongest weapon, after June 1921, was a wage-cut. Gas workers lost 1s a shift, 12½% in October, then ½d an hour in April 1922 and another ½d in May; scavengers lost 4s in January 1922 and 1s for every five points drop in the cost of living index; slaughter-men and harbour-men lost 1s, while public health and lighting men lost 5%. There were still anomalies: the lavatory attendant with as little as a 3s rise in 1920, or the gas clerkess who received 40s weekly while her male colleagues earned 65s. Only professional staff had reasonable salaries: the burgh surveyor earned £350 per annum and the architect £450.

The private sector was even more restless and strikes were almost fashionable. In 1918 alone some 5,875,000 days were lost in the United Kingdom and the 1919 industrial courts did little to improve matters. There were many strikes in Perth. Moulders wanted a forty-hour week, while the Textile Workers' Union at Garvie and Deas argued for a rise. The September-October 1919 rail strike was much more damaging than the other strikes in that over 1,000 National Union of Railwaymen men lived in Perth, but most people took the advice of the Government to carry on working. In 1920, the bakers asked for a rise of £5 a week, while clerks in banks and the General Accident Insurance Company had more modest ambitions. At the end of the year, 200 builders went on strike. In May 1922, postmen demanded better conditions. Nevertheless, as with the rail upsets, it was the coal strikes of October 1920 and April 1921 that really hurt. No wonder 'Cyrnicus' could write in the *Perthshire Advertiser*: 'Let them all strike! The public is sick of the agitators' talk and bombast!' The situation was not much better at Messrs Frank S Sandeman's at Stanley Mills in March 1919. There a girl refused to join the Textile Workers' Union who were vigorously pursuing a policy of closed-shop. Working in the Mechanics'

Department, the Textile Union was no use to her, and in any case, none of the mechanics were union members. Five hundred women came out on strike and attacked the girl after work. Police and mechanics escorted her through a baying mob blowing trumpets, rattling tins and booing. The *Constitutional* declared: 'Police Draw Batons at Stanley'. When the girl joined another union, the mechanics came out in protest. Two months later, seven workers were fined in Perth Sheriff Court for intimidation. Just as these proceedings were underway, the Scottish Trades Union Congress met in Perth and Rushworth of the Dyers' Union publicly distanced himself from the 'Red Clyde.'

That summer, the wages of railwaymen were cut by 5s, and bakers, although threatened with a 17s cut, ended up with a 10s cut and an hour added to their working week. In August 1920, the bleachers at Messrs Lumsden and Mackenzie at Huntingtower, Pitcairngreen and Stormontfield and those at Messrs James Burt-Marshall at Luncarty, demanded a closed-shop, and when refused, went on strike. In Bankfoot village, two of them were arrested for breach of the peace and bailed at £3. By 4 August, Almondbank and Luncarty were 'lively' as seven hundred formed pickets at the two firms. At the latter, 237 workers enrolled in the Dyers' Union and demanded 70s for men and 50s for women. Negotiations with the union convinced Major Hodge of Burt-Marshall to recognise the union, but this was rejected by the Dyers' Union who wanted to tie the closed-shop argument to a wage rise. A week later the union demand went up by 8s although the firm offered 4s. By now Luncarty was a hot-bed of unrest and in a Luncarty to Perth march there were seventeen arrests. The Dyers' Union suggested a rent strike and the firm responded by sending each striker a warning that unless there was a speedy settlement, they might have to relinquish their tied houses. That night there were meetings on the North Inch and at the High Street Port as rumour spread that the firm was hiring new men. Then followed a seven-hour meeting between Hodge and Dougherty of the Dyers' Union. The *Constitutional* on 25 August claimed that a settlement was certain because of pressure from the Master Bleachers' Association and hinted that men would receive 4s and women 2s backdated to 1 August.

Details of what had gone on behind the scenes now emerged. Twenty policemen had been used when the two firms had asked for protection, there had been twenty arrests and the Dyers' Union had dropped their demand for a closed-shop. Then came the legal assessment before Sheriff Boswell on 13 September. Five Ruthvenfield and three Pitcairngreen workers, one of the former being a James Turner DCM, MM, Cross of St George of Russia, were all found guilty and fined. Although it had been a good-humoured strike, there were other casualties. A few were not reinstated and the Luncarty general manager retired.

The post-war period began rather ominously for Scotland in the economic field as control of so many industries was now in English hands. While capital growth was slow in Perth, by March 1920, the Government allowed the Exchange Rate to fluctuate and they were forced into a new War Loan and a Finance Act which raised income tax. When the post-war slump began during 1921-1922, exports and production levels fell until cotton was only a third of the 1913 level, coal production was down by forty million tons and two million were idle in the United Kingdom. The old staple industries had started to contract in the face of a sluggish international economy and fiercer competition. This was obvious to Perth dyers as within months of the end of the war, German dyes had again captured the market.

Meanwhile, Frank E Eastman had rearranged working patterns at the North British Dye Works. Work now started at 8 a.m rather than 6 a.m. There was a Works' Council and new stress on modern advertising. There was even an innovative three-day Conference for Managers from London, Edinburgh, Dublin, Manchester, Liverpool, Newcastle, Bristol and Birmingham, at which it was agreed to expand agencies, purchase more vans, improve rail transit and advertise. Suddenly, the workers, afraid of losing their war bonuses, went on strike and won their claim for 5s for men and 4s for women, provided that they made no wage demands for a year and promised to accept pre-war rates if the cost of living fell. Eastman tried hard to conciliate the union. He took on the unemployed Campbell workers, rejected overtime and opened the Tulloch Institute to women employees. The *Perthshire Advertiser* on 24 May 1919 stated that the demands of all workers had been met. A dyer now had 57s, a skilled man, 51s, an unskilled, 47s and women, 40s. Yet within three months the union was back asking for 5s 6d on pre-war rates and 25% on the present rate as the cost of living was rising again. The September 1919 rail strike worsened the situation and the firm, in October, conceded a further 4s to men and 2s to women for an increase in the cost of living.

By 1920, some 2,000 employees were in the Dyers' Union, a far cry from the sixty-seven of 1917. On 6 March, the North British Dye Works closed at noon and a War Memorial tablet bearing the names of the sixty-one dead, thirty-nine of them from the Black Watch, was unveiled by Mrs Eastman in the presence of the Duke of Atholl and Sir Robert Moncrieffe, but no members of the Pullars family were present. In an emotional delivery, Frank Eastman told how they had gone out 'for honour because Britain had given its word to Belgium ... they realised that their choice was either slavery or death ... they were fighting for a civilization.' He recalled the 470 men who had gone to war, the fourteen decorations they had been awarded and the 12.9% who fell. The piper played 'The Flowers of the Forest' and the wreaths were carried by Sergeant Anderson MM, and Company Sergeant Major Mitchell DCM.

At this point Eastman disclosed details of the firm's new pension and sickness and holiday schemes. A worker unable to continue working would receive a pension based on 2½d in the pound in wages multiplied by the number of years worked. Sickness pay of 8s would be paid to men and 6s to women for eight weeks and then another eight weeks at half-scale. Holidays with a week's pay would be granted to those who had spent four years with the firm. The editor of the *Constitutional* considered it 'a most generous proposal as the Company provides all the funds.' It is doubtful if Eastman fully appreciated the future cost given that it was an ageing workforce, or the loss in profits due to the October 1920 coal strike. At any rate, a fall in the cost of living in December saw wages reduced. The union did not like this and complained to Sir D Shakelton, Arbiter, and when he found for the workers, the money was restored.

The year 1921 was promising. Although short of some materials, all the men were back from the war and the Works' Council was a distinct success. But merging with Campbells meant that the

North British Dye Works was now legally responsible for the 26,000 claims, totalling £105,000, for damages which were due to go to court. Disaster came even before the merger costs could be assimilated with another coal strike in April. By 18 April, National Defence Force troops were in Perth, about two hundred at the Old Infirmary, and others, with fixed bayonets, at the railway station.

Some 1,500 workers from Pullars had to be laid off and by the end of the month there was only a week's supply of coal left in stock. On 2 May 1921, the *Constitutional* headline announced: 'Coal Crisis in Perth' amid warnings that 2,900 would be idle if the North British Dye Works had to close down. The Dyers' Union appealed to the miners and the railwaymen and a special permit gave them enough coal for a three-day week. Well might the *Constitutional* report on 11 May that the outlook was not so bright. Then, just as the North British Dye Works was on the point of closing at the end of the month, four hundred tons of French coal arrived with the promise of American shipments soon afterwards.

Unbelievably, the firm staggered into further difficulties a few months later. On 3 December 1921, the *Perthshire Advertiser* informed the people of Perth of a crisis in the dying industry because of an Employers' Association and Dyers' Union agreement in Manchester to give full pay for a forty-hour week, with a sliding scale down to thirty-three hours. Eastman refused to accept this and came up with the suggestion that the workers lose pay for the first seven hours' work and that he retain the right to dismiss. Trade was 'dull' in early December and the firm paid off two hundred. The argument was basic: Eastman wanted the workers to lose pay on seven hours' work until January 1922. The union refused to agree to this and wanted a guaranteed thirty-three hours, which the firm, in its turn, refused. A week later another fifty were paid off and the *Perthshire Advertiser* reported on 10 December that 250 dye-workers were unemployed. The union was forced to yield and accept the firm's New Agreement that all new employees serve a four-year probationary period during which time they would only receive 75% of the established wage, and thereafter, the 'set wage' which carried with it the promise to work thirty-two hours every six months without pay.

By now most of the workers felt that they had lost all the post-war gains at a stroke and Rushworth, on behalf of the union, could only weakly suggest that he have a say in dismissals. He publicly asked how much money the firm was saving and how many workers had been paid off. He accused Eastman of talking about dismissing workers and violating agreements. Eastman's reply was short: 'An employer must retain the right to lay off during an acute depression and we cannot give guarantees.' It was clear to most of Perth that Pullars was in a 'great depression' and the hundred clerical members of the Scottish Clerks' Union wisely accepted the seven-hour pay cut. The Dyers' Union came back with more sensible proposals: in return for a forty-hour week and no dismissals, each man would accept a cut of 8s to 12s for three months. The firm did its best too. In February 1922, it cut dry-cleaning charges and in August, dyeing charges, thereby upsetting its cash flow. In fact, the matter was not fully settled until August 1923. Ominously, soup kitchens were in action again in Perth.

P and P Campbell had faced similar problems in 1918. The working week was cut to forty-seven hours, ex-soldiers were rehired and rises were granted all round. Although they had plenty of dyes, no plant had been upgraded in the previous five years. They were to pay a terrible price for the war years on 20 May 1919 when the Perth Dye Works was destroyed in what the *Perthshire Advertiser* described as 'Perth's most destructive fire, an unparalleled conflagration.' Those left idle, but soon to be employed by Pullars, numbered 370 and the damage cost £250,000. The blaze was so serious that the nearby Moncrieff Glass Works was abandoned. The fire had threatened the city, the Wallace and Balhousie Works, and the Barracks. Fortunately, there was a speedy solution to the damage caused by the fire when the two firms, Campbells and Pullars, amalgamated. P W and E Campbell retired and Lieutenant Peter Campbell Junior joined Pullars as a director.

Despite his problems Eastman launched a building campaign in September 1919 and the first purely cement-reinforced building in Perth emerged with electric lifts and a 78,000 gallon concrete water-tank on the roof. It was fireproof.

Perth's other major industries also had their post-war troubles. Thomson's Fair City Dyeworks suffered a pay strike in May 1919, followed by the rail strike in September which hit them badly. Cleverly, the firm set about storing coal for the next strike which came in October 1920, but they had already decided to move from dyeing to more profitable cleaning, especially laundering, as the colours being used were not as bright as pre-war. With the third coal strike in April 1921, their dyeing ceased altogether. The shift to cleaning proved to be a wise one as the cost of dyes was up twenty times on the 1913 prices and bag-wash had an enormous advantage in that demand did not vary from season to season.

Garvie and Deas had a constant struggle in July 1919 with the Textile Workers' Union, while Moncrieff Glass Works repeatedly had to lay off its 500 workers as lack of coal damaged its ovens. The Foundry, which had installed electricity in February 1920, found itself heavily in debt. Shields' Wallace Works entered 1919 with a massive profit of £18,729 and awarded a retrospective pay rise of 7s to men, 5s to women and 2s 6d to girls, back-dated to December 1919. Then after a damaging coal strike came the rise in the cost of living and the workers demanded a 10s rise, which they felt the firm could well afford as the 1920 profit level was £19,863. Actually short of female labour, the firm had no option but to grant the rise, taking care to point out that increases therefore meant wages were 125% over the pre-war wage level when bonuses and war wages together were taken into account. By 1921, the firm felt itself to be in crisis as the linen trade disintegrated all over the country. The April 1921 coal strike led to a three-day week and 1922 was a year of considerable anxiety. Coates' Balhousie Works was in a parallel position. It began 1919 by a return to a fifty-hour week and because jute and wool were in short supply, they soon found themselves with three hundred workers on short time. From then on it was nothing but disaster. There was a coal strike in September 1919, a rail strike in October 1919, another coal strike in April 1921, a 12½ payout in September 1921, and in January 1922, the collapse of the carpet market and a jute depression.

The State too also had to unwind in the reconstruction era of 1918-1922. Although the transition from war to peace was not entirely smooth, many were glad to see the powers of the State emasculated. They remembered only too well the ruthless ferocity with which it had fought to survive. In 1919 the Ministries of Reconstruction, Information, Blockade, Munitions, National Service, Food and Shipping were dismantled. The War Cabinet was soon dissolved and the coalmines and railways returned to their owners. The Addison Scheme was brought to an end and the Corn Production Act 1917, which guaranteed prices and a minimum wage, was repealed and by 1920 much of the wartime governmental machinery had been dismantled. But enough was retained: the Ministries of Health, Labour, Transport and The Defence of the Realm Act, lying dormant as it were, to be reactivated if required in the future.

With an enormously swollen electorate, the General Election of 1918 was considered important. Campaigning began early on 14 November and four weeks later the nation went to the polls. Despite its anomalies - the limited age-level for women and the lack of male residential qualifications - the Representation of the People Act 1918 represented considerable political changes. In Perth, W Young, Coalition, was returned unopposed, one of the 537 successful candidates for the Coalition-Liberals. This released a wave of political debate in the city, first on the advantages, if any, of proportional representation, and then of the Soviet system. Concerning the latter, at a public meeting in the City Hall, 1,016 (63.5%) voted against the Soviet system and only 590 in its favour. But there were already signs that the political spectrum was polarising as the Right and Left became more extreme. In 1920, the National Democratic Party and the Communist Party of Great Britain were formed. Police suspicions of the Communist Party were soon stirred. This was reflected in the Town Council who were less than helpful to the Independent Labour Party's fraternal greetings to comrades in the USSR. In contrast was the Town Council's attitude to the Labour Party, backed by the powerful Trades' Labour Council whose applications for use of the North Inch were usually upheld. Generally, the feeling in the city was that the Liberals were running out of steam - there were no Pullar members in the Liberal Club - and that the Unionists were the coming men. Sadly, extremism was lurking in the air and many expected a clash in the future between Capital and Labour.

Newspapers were among the first to analyse the war, the Peace Conference and the Treaty of Versailles to see if there were any lessons to be learnt. However, the interest of their readers, now numbering 5,500,000 nationally, were changing and there was a desire for escapism, especially through magazines and films. Holidays were an obvious example and the 'Perth for Holidays' campaign was financed by the City of Perth Advertising Fund. Formats had changed with photos regularly featuring even in advertisements. Violent acts such as the Amritsar massacre and the deaths of 379 people in India in April 1919 were handled almost dramatically. On the other hand, breach of promise cases were rare in newspapers after 1921. Visits by VIPs were much applauded: Lloyd George; Admiral Beatty; Ramsay Macdonald and Crown Prince Hirohito, but more space was devoted to local war heroes like Captain Robert Halley DFC and Bar, MM, who went on to fight the Afghans in 1919. Naturally, old topics remained, the safety of drinking water from the Tay for instance. Unfortunately, Perth's sewage problem was no nearer a solution than a decade before. Newspapers handled the topic of women rather differently as well in the post-war period. Dr Elsie Inglis who died in 1917, and Edith Cavell who died in 1915, were cast as role models. The Sex Disqualification (Removal) Act 1919 lifted the barriers and women achieved many 'firsts' in this period: first Justice of the Peace, Mrs Summers; first to the Bar, Ivy Williams; first Cabinet Minister, Margaret Bondfield, and by 1921, the 1911 level of professional women had doubled. Oddly enough, women lost out in almost every area into which they had entered so enthusiastically during the war.

As if to emphasise their partnership with men, women's fashions turned to the 'boyish look' achieved by a Bob, Shingle or Eton Crop hairstyle under a cloche hat. With a straight silhouette to hide bust and hips, there was no stiff corset nor starched petticoat and the skirt was well above the knee. The more outlandish were the 'Amazons' who smoked in public, drank beer and had bi-sexual names like Jo and Billie. All, of course, were designed to shock. Men were more practical as demobilisation had stimulated a demand for ready-made clothing, tweed jacket, flannel trousers with a sharp crease, bow tie and bright socks. They too, however, had their outlandish group, 'The Nut'. Always fed-up, 'The Nut' was an elegant idler who smoked heavily and loved cars and was slightly effeminate. Like all extremes in fashion, 'The Nut' and the 'Amazon' did not last.

Most sports, amusements and pastimes of the pre-war period survived, but the hard lines of class divisions had been blurred and the order of priority was constantly changing. Perth was still essentially a cricket city, although football was fast becoming a serious challenge. Unfortunately, junior football had an image-problem, shown by John Keay as secretary of the Perthshire Junior Football Association, when he appealed for police presence to curb the unruly conduct of some spectators on Saturday afternoons. Tennis received a boost when it was recommended as ideal for girls and tennis courts were prepared for the North Inch.

The North Inch was once again the weekend social centre for the city, particularly with its Sunday Band Concerts, but now there was a refreshment pavilion. Bowling was equally popular and a green was built on the South Inch. The Town Council were still conscious of their need to protect the Inches and although they allowed a skating pond on the South Inch, they refused a whippet-racing arena. Open-air dancing was also refused. While bigger cities had their dancehalls called Palais or Mecca or Locarno, Perth had none of these and dancers had to be content with the use of hired halls. It was this lack of specialised facilities that persuaded the Town Council to allow the swimming baths to be used for gymnastics and the City Hall for badminton and boxing. Inevitably, many ambitious plans fell through, usually through lack of money. One expanding interest was flying. Many men had served in the Royal Flying Corps/Royal Air Force during the war and Scotland had finished up with no fewer than thirty airbases and having made 2,000 aircraft in its factories. Most schoolboys could describe in detail the structure of a DH9, BE2C, FE2b, Avro540k and the exploits of Canadian air-ace, Colonel Billy Barker VC, who visited the city in July 1922. Various attempts were made by Captain Andrews of Leuchars Aerial Photos Ltd, Edinburgh and Jones Flying Company to arrange flights from the North Inch. Motoring too had soared in popularity, and despite its negative side with car thefts, accidents and traffic congestion, it was here to stay. The Town Council responded with more road signs, better road classifications, bigger garages, more petrol stations, more one-way streets and better road surfaces.

The greatest change in the post-war period in the field of entertainment was, of course, the cinema. Most people had attended the cinema during the war and the picture-going habit continued. Although the public barely realised it, there was constant change. For instance, it was soon obvious that the Cinematograph Film Act 1909 was obsolete and this led to the 1919 closure of the Corona Picture House in the High Street to become a shop. The city was left with just four cinemas until in 1921, the Theatre was given a licence, making five again. BB Pictures Ltd had hoped to open a new cinema at the corner of King Edward Street and St John's Place, but exit problems nipped it in the bud. BB Pictures Ltd was wound up soon afterwards and a new company, BB Pictures, took over. Unfortunately, the BB Cinema suffered a £12,000 fire which served to show the need for the new Celluloid and Cinematograph Act 1922. However, Currie Enterprises Ltd had leased a site at the corner of Foundry Lane and Kinnoull Street in May 1921 and within a year the Alhambra Cinema was open. The city now had six cinemas.

Physically, the city of Perth had hardly altered by the year 1922 apart from a little development to the north and west. Its population had actually fallen to the 33,000 mark due to the fact that many had gone off to seek work in munitions. As for the city's famous dyeing industry, it was already in decline. While marriages, and consequently, births were on the increase, the outward flow of emigrants to Canada had already started again. This new generation of pioneers was different to the pre-1914 variety. They had lost the passion of patriotism and the mystique of Empire had gone. So indeed had the city's rural quality. Little Dunning Markets were challenged in law by eighteen shop-owners under the Sale of Food Order 1920, and the stalls slowly dwindled year-by-year. The noisy cries of young street-traders were also a thing of the past. There was now a bye-law which forbade any young person under the age of seventeen from selling wares in the streets. There were still heavy carthorses, but the pony-traps and dogcarts had vanished and there were fewer corner horse-troughs every year. Many of the old, medieval closes, pends and vennels were closed up or torn down in a city that was changing itself for the motorcar. There were far fewer trams and lots more buses and there were even people complaining about the nuisance value of the old tramlines. Dress had changed considerably and seemed freer and less restricted and was certainly less conventional. Women could be seen in long skirts with collar and tie playing tennis in public.

In a city with no nightclubs and where its citizens did not sip cocktails nor listen to jazz, the cinema had become the great trendsetter. The young fashioned their dress, manners and even lifestyle on their celluloid heroes and heroines. Even language was changing to the trans-Atlantic monosyllables. For the older generation, there were many irritations: short skirts and smoking in public, both deliberately intended to shock and affront. Much seemed to have been lost, and they began to look back, with faulty memory, to the halcyon days of pre-1914.

ON FLOWS THE TAY

How then did the First World War affect the city of Perth? Was there social change, and if so, how much and in what areas of life?

Given that Perth is only a small part of the national spectrum it is clear that the city did not experience 'total war', however defined, in the years 1914-1922. There was no destruction of property through enemy action by air raids or invasion. Indeed, there was little in the city by 1922 that indicated that a major conflict had been fought, apart, that is, from a rusting hulk of a tank at Buckie Braes on which children played on Sunday afternoons and a few field guns tucked away in odd corners of the city's parks.

The military's presence in the city had been quickly removed. No longer were there practice-trenches on the North Inch or cavalry lines on the South Inch. Halls requisitioned as recreation-clubs and flats reserved for officers and men reverted to their former roles. The flood of khaki uniforms in the High Street had ebbed away and the Regular Army was out in India fighting the Afghans. Only a small force of specialist and rather elderly instructors was left in the barracks. The City Hall was no longer required for patriotic concerts or hysterical recruiting rallies and the swimming baths had restored entrance priority once again to schoolchildren. The river, as ever, flowed on, and as usual, sublimely unaware of man's follies. Only Kinnoull Hill showed signs of abuse. There was not a fully developed birch or ash left on the slopes. All had been cut down by the Canadian Forestry Corps. But this had been the case once before in 1811 during the Napoleonic Wars when Kinnoull Hill had been denuded of forest. It had recovered then and the Town Council were determined it would recover again.

The war then for Perth, and one would suspect for most of Scotland, could be described as 'a limited war' only. Many people had been only marginally involved, especially if they had no loved ones at the Front and had enough cash to buy the little extras in what a later generation was to call the Black Market. Middle-class people could still have their fortnight's holiday in August at Strathpeffer, while reading of newspapers with patriotic interest remained their sole contribution to the nation's fight. Many, no doubt, salvaged their consciences with hefty donations to a host of war charities that sprang up almost nightly in the first few months of the war.

Not very different were working-class people who did not have a husband, son, father or brother in uniform. Most had more money during the war than they ever had before and many enjoyed themselves. Clothes may have been expensive and food even scarce, but there was always a nice gramophone to buy or a trip by train to Broughty Ferry. Others, in vivid contrast, were plunged into deep gloom by the death of a husband at Loos or a son on the Somme, separation for years by service abroad or the breakdown of a marriage. These were sad situations, which however, do not add up to social change of any magnitude.

Compared to other stages in the city's recorded past, the First World War was not a period of great hardship for Perth. In the Middle Ages, a time when the city was protected by a wall and a moat, Perth was the scene of constant pillage by English armies. In 1644, a savage battle, Tippermuir, was fought on the outskirts of Perth when hundreds of Perth citizens were killed, a far higher proportion of the population than in 1914-1918. Indeed, 'total war' descended on Perth as bubonic plague swept the survivors and competing armies repeatedly took and lost the city. Even a cursory inspection of the Kirk Session and Presbytery minutes record dozens of rapes and murders as anarchy took hold of the land. During the latter part of the 18th century and the early part of the 19th century, long French Revolutionary and Napoleonic Wars drained the city of its young men as recruiting parties and press-gangs screened the area for fresh blood. This sometimes meant an abductee's unrecorded death in the Spanish sierras, or after long years of service being dumped ashore at Portsmouth and left to find his way back to Perth to spend the rest of his days begging in the streets. To fight in an army that used flogging as a stimulant and had never heard of pensions or allowances was far worse than the First World War. The people of Perth in 1796 knew what 18th century conscription meant, and hence the militia riots against recruitment. The corn riots of the same period, when crowds of local citizens forced their way into warehouses to find food, are largely forgotten. Clearly, these represent 'total war' and yet none of these events were industrial. But they were all fought without restraint and they involved everybody. That is the nub of 'total war'.

If this is so, why then do so many regard 1914-1918 as an enormous gulf in the flow of history? Why do many see it as a watershed in their personal lives, a view even shared by those whose involvement in the First World War was so marginal as to be almost laughable? One answer is that everybody and every society needs a benchmark in life, something by which change can be measured, however fast or slow it may be. And that is what 1914-1918 provides. It becomes a peg on which to hang memories, and before long myths evolve. An elderly survivor proved the point. She had had 'a good life' on 5s 6d a week. Yet, for this, she had to work fifty-one hours. Her wage was so low that she never had new clothes, just hand-me-downs, could not afford a room of her own but shared with three other girls, was usually hungry by the middle of the week, her favourite pastimes were the cinema at 2d, the waxworks at 1d and walking. These were 'the good old days' to her. The soldiers were no different. Even those who had lost an arm at Festubert or an eye at Gaza, harboured memories, in the main, of comradeship, shared laughs and comical incidents. The pain, horror and fear had been largely blotted out by their faulty memories. Gone were the thousands of hours of boredom, the hundreds of hours of humiliation and the few hours of sheer terror. Instead, they remembered the night they got drunk at Arras or the strange sight of a broken piece of funereal sculpture at Ypres. These stories repeated again and again in Ex-Servicemen's Clubs and British Legion Nights were the seedbed for a forest of myths.

One of these myths, understandably, was that of a lost generation of talent and leadership lying in the mud of Flanders. By the 1920s and 1930s this had become almost a 'scientific fact'. In reality, no matter how much grief and sadness we may feel for the countless millions who died, it is simply just not true, although it is easy to believe as one stands at a Memorial and listens to the tearful pipe-lament, 'The Flowers of the Forest'. The facts, however, are otherwise.

The economic problem facing society in the post-war period was not due to the deaths of so many, but to the iron laws of supply-and-demand. The world was changing and with it came new problems and challenges. In terms of numbers, Perth lost about 1,000 men, 10% of those who had served, two were blinded for life, five were hospitalised for mental treatment, 263 were maimed requiring years of convalescent treatment: some 1,260 lives ruined by war. Harsh though it sounds, this can be seen as a fair price for a limited war. It was the same with the population of Perth as a whole: the 36,000 of 1910 had fallen to 33,000 by 1922. A sign of 'total war'?

The Golden Book at St John's Kirk, Perth

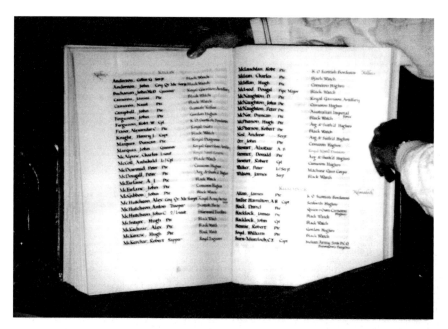

Names of Perth's War Dead in the Golden Book

By the very nature of her major industry, dyeing, Perth had always had a high degree of social mobility. The pre-war custom was for a dyer to leave Perth and work in London, Paris or Berlin to perfect his skills and then return to a promoted post in Perth. Every confrontation between management and labour produced 'encouraged-to-leave' *quittals* and a passage to Montreal. Even during the period 1910 to 1914, large numbers of tradesmen left Perth for Canada. It is a mistake to assume that it was war that stopped this flow in 1914. In reality, it was stopped by a wave of unemployment which hit the Canadian Pacific Railway, the main hiring agency for emigrants from Perth, early in July 1914. Furthermore, a fair number of domestic workers left Perth to go west to Glasgow or south to London to work as *munitionettes* where they married and settled down. Lastly, the birth rate between 1910 and 1922 was never high, but it certainly rose later.

Changes in legislation destroyed Perth's rural quality far more than war did. Little Dunning was doomed when legislation was introduced to meet the complaints of shopkeepers who lost trade because stallholders paid no rates. Street trading went the same way. This had nothing to do with the war, but the simple facts that the Town Council lost out on rate payments and the police were concerned by the amount of stolen goods that changed hands at the stalls, often later retrieved from gypsy-hawkers. The pony and trap as well as the dogcarts were simply outmoded by changes in the city's transport arrangements. Trams and an increasing number of buses were unsuitable companions for dogcarts, which traditionally delivered the milk in Perth.

The factor which most influenced Perth's push into the 20th century was not the First World War but the motorcar. Horse transport in Perth finally ended in 1905 and by 1911 even the tram was on its way to being replaced by the bus. These changes were gradual and sometimes the different forms existed side-by-side for years. But change came faster after 1908 when Henry Ford's Model T and his 1913 Detroit car assembly line promised mass-production and a cheaper process. Some, usually the elderly, thought the car a passing fad which would never replace the horse. After all, did the Locomotive Act not require a vehicle to be preceded by a man with a red flag if crossing a bridge? And was the maximum speed in Perth in 1902 not only 2 mph? The 1903 Motorcar Act which increased the maximum speed to 20 mph was the spur that was needed.

Perth, like most cities, responded quickly. Specialised shops appeared selling spare-parts for enthusiastic do-it-yourself fanatics, while local businesses opened garages in the centre of the city to win the increasingly expensive repair market. As more cars and buses took to the streets, the Town Council realised that the medieval streets of Perth were quite inadequate. They had to be made wider, with better surfaces and safer pavements. Town planners devised complicated schemes to divert traffic away from the city and the concept of ring roads was born. Not only new streets emerged, but signposts and notices and even another new concept, the one-way street. Amidst this mass of change it was clear that traffic police would have to be appointed and by 1913 this had been done. The total effect was incredible. Old and narrow pends, closes, vennels and wynds were closed and the medieval history of Perth began to disappear. Dress was influenced as the fashion world seized the idea of producing motoring coats and driving scarves. Newspapers were altered as motoring columns and car-sale advertisements ousted traditional space reserved for School Board and Presbytery Reports. Language too was given a new range of terms: speedster; road hog and scorching. Before long, even the technical jargon had joined everyday speech: clutch, gears and windscreen. Law itself was influenced as traffic violations crept steadily up the criminal calendar and new offences such as car theft and licence fraud appeared. Its very popularity, especially among the young, obscured the fact that the motorcar was reshaping the city and this had nothing to do with the war.

There was another agency destined to alter the city and in many ways it was quite unexpected. Although animated photographs were shown in Aberdeen as far back as 1896, few could possibly have believed the scope of its technological development over the following decade. Many regarded the film as little more than a sophisticated version of the 1848 Diorama. As such, it was simply an entertaining toy. But, invention backed by massive capital investment dictated otherwise. Society did not realise that it was about to experience a revolution. It was clearly so in Perth by 1911. Roller rinks and music halls were already closing down in the city and the scramble to build cinemas had begun. The rough-and-ready image of the cinema, which so many claim was eradicated by the war, disappeared in Perth by 1913 when the city could already sport five picture-houses. Everybody was keen to taste the 'visual experience' of the movies, especially as it developed so rapidly. As early as 1914, Perth enjoyed éclair-coloured films. Like everything else there were fads, but the greatest change was the portrayal of current events. The Newsreel, which attracted huge crowds during the war years, was born. By 1922, the cinema was the leading trendsetter for the young. It shaped their attitude to language and a fashion for Americanisms, their dress, their manners and their lifestyle. Their heroes were no longer those of the *Boys' Own* pre-1914 image, but the celluloid screen star packaged in Hollywood. Cinema going was now a habit, a form of escapism for a visually hungry public little influenced by the war.

One result of war was to give thousands of ordinary men and women a chance to experience the thrills of flying which was becoming less and less a purely aristocratic pursuit. This did not, however, make its promised headway in Perth. The Town Council assiduously protected the Inches, as they had always done, and watched with a tolerant eye as sports, pastimes and amusements changed with the times. The divisions between working-class and middle-class amusements tended to blur, not because of the war's influence on democratisation, but because, especially in 1922, there was more money around. Cricket was still king, but football was more exciting. Walking competitions, roller-skating, pierrots, waxworks and glee clubs had all gone. Vaudeville and minstrel shows as well as menageries and circuses were fading; dominoes and billiards were gaining respect. Indoors, the gramophone had replaced the piano, and outdoors, tennis had overtaken croquet.

The effect of the war on class-structure is almost impossible to assess given the lack of effective data. But several points do seem clear. Scotland had never had the snobbish attitude to class that is found in England and this is just as true of Perth. Whatever class differences there were in 1910, they were still there in 1922, except that they were less sharply defined. Differences became increasingly subtle. For instance, while it was comparatively easy to determine class by dress in 1910, it was less easy to do so in 1922. Myths abound in this sociological jungle. For example, there are no indications that the landed class around Perth went into decline. Furthermore, the social polarisation that some claim grew after the war had its roots in the years 1911-1912. Social life, which had decayed around 1915, had fully recovered by 1919, at least in Perth. The city may have lost its leading family, the Pullars, but the gap had been quickly filled by the Eastmans. The departure of the former had more to do with the challenge of trade union growth rather than the war itself. Perth had no hard-faced men who did well out of the war. Neither did it have a neurotic generation of 'gin-swilling flappers' and the Turkey Trot and Tango were both known as early as 1912. Even jazz was available, but not popular, in 1911. At the same time, any class homogeneity generated by the war, either in civilian or military life, did not last long. For most people in Perth, 'respectability' as had been pre-1914, was inviolate. A great deal of the social change which commentators saw and recorded in London was blissfully unknown in Perth.

Not many realise that council housing stretches back to the 1850s when Town Councils were given limited powers of intervention. These were systematically extended in 1868, 1875 and 1890 when slum clearances, redevelopment, re-housing and cheap loans appeared. The concept of a Garden City was already well known in 1898 and the idea of a green belt was widely discussed by 1914. In Perth the post-war housing was in response to an emergency and pressure from local deputations. Little had, in fact, been done by 1922. Nonetheless, one can say that it was the Housing and Town Planning Act of 1909, rather than the war itself, which generated housing changes in Perth. Attempts had been made in Perth to regulate building standards as far back as 1878 and some low-rent housing had been available as early as 1890. Slums were still in existence after 1918, mainly because landlords had no money for improvements and building costs were too high.

Dress is perhaps the most commonly presented evidence of the effect of war and it would certainly appear so when one considers the pre-1914 woman so grandly corseted and bedecked with great hats and feathers. In contrast we have the post-war boyish look with its almost sexless-outline designed for freer, less restricted, less conventional, more relaxed wear. Yet, when one considers the dress of men pre-war, one realises that strict formality was already fading. In Perth lounge suits had become fashionable with the appearance of George V in 1910, and formal attire, in the shape of top hat and morning suit, was reserved for professional men. It was clear that formality, like spats, was ebbing away. In the post-war period men proved their pragmatic nature by making extensive use of ready-made clothing. Khaki, owed its wide use, not to 1914-1918, as many believe, but to the Boer War of 1899-1901. There has been considerable writing about women's designs and fashions reflecting the need for easy movement in munitions' work, driving Red Cross ambulances, but much of this ignores the fact that dress, for women, is a never-ending whirl of change, having remarkably little to do with national events. Magazine drawings and film excerpts inspired the dress changes of many.

Drink is probably Scotland's oldest social illness and many forget that the Edwardian pub was often open from 10 a.m to 11 p.m. The numerous attempts to curb the drinking excesses of the public go far back into the 19th century and continued long after 1918. They were all unsuccessful. Vested interests in the drink trade were far too strong and even the State could not resolve the issue. The fact that legislation cannot curb drinkers is inescapable. The drinker will always be the drinker. This is shown in Perth by the failure of the modest temperance reforms of 1920. In fact, by 1923, despite the great reduction in the number of *howffs*, the situation was as bad as the early 1900s. By 1923, however, there is some evidence that there was a correlation between drinking and unemployment.

An interesting feature about health is that it did not appear to suffer much during the war. Many argue that this is because of improvements in brain surgery and blood transfusion techniques stimulated by the war. In Perth, however, there is clear evidence that more money was spent on food and with better nutrition the level of malnutrition fell drastically. The State's awareness of the importance of personal health goes back to 1911 when it realised that bad health and squalor were the product of poverty rather than idleness and immorality. Greater participation on the part of the State was inescapable as medical costs started their long climb upwards with the introduction of electric treatment, X-rays and massage, together with salaries for specialists like bacteriologists and radiologists. Thus, the founding of the Scottish Board of Health, although logical and inevitable, is nonetheless a revolution.

Health consciousness was not new and neither were health foods, but in the post-war era they received greater prominence. This is particularly true in relation to venereal disease. There had been an awareness for a long time of VD being related to social mobility which during the war had free rein. The spread of the disease at this point was due to the movement of masses of virile young men from their sexual partners rather than any specific decline in morality as the Church liked to proclaim. A greater threat to the community, however, was tuberculosis, a disease not entirely understood in 1922, except that it seemed to be related to inadequate housing. Disease, as statisticians were beginning to realise, comes in waves and when any population's stability is disturbed, the risk increases. Naturally, war is such a time. Mental health did improve after the war at a time when more forms of psychosis emerged in breakdowns and post-traumatic stresses. Medical practitioners were made aware of the need for mental hygiene and this seems to have been accompanied by greater sensitivity in handling patients.

Child welfare has attracted considerable attention and many have argued that this is entirely due to the First World War. This is not so. In Perth, a school nurse, free issues of toothpaste, boots and spectacles all date from 1908 and 1909. The foundation of the local Nursery Association in 1908 introduced a policy of diets and special classes, a cooking depot, holiday homes, physical education and more butter and milk in the food. By 1922, this had been extended to cover cleaning stations, home visits for infants, a child clinic and child welfare officers. While all these measures did not remove bad teeth, head lice and impetigo, it did reduce their levels.

The First World War placed every religious denomination in Perth in a dilemma. How could God allow this? Where were the concepts of love and forgiveness? The Church could not explain the need for suffering and turned to its traditional attitude: man is selfish, intemperate and impure. Some Perth clerics who taught that the Kaiser was, literally, the Anti-Christ, called, with a strange logic, for a Holy War. Many in Perth declared these warlike clerics hypocrites as they urged the use of revenge air attacks and even dum-dum bullets. The majority of clergymen responded as best they could. They served as chaplains at the Front or as special constables at home. Some lost their sons in battle. When one of their number, on grounds of conscience, exempted himself from the Military Service Act 1916, he attracted a great deal of personal abuse. The clergy appeared inadequate to many compared to the host of mediums, palmists, fortune-tellers and crystal gazers who sold amulets, charms, horoscopes and talismans to a gullible public.

Formal religion was in decline everywhere and the Church, in Perth, had begun to lose its authority long before 1914. Although the working classes had had little contact with the Church for decades, it was the slackening among the middle-class churchgoers that caused the most comment during the war. It was hardly surprising. The Victorian Sabbath just could not compete with the modern bicycle, motorbike and motorcar. Thus, there are reasons other than the war for the decline of faith in Perth: industrialisation and the evolution of an overtly materialistic society. Then there was the growth of socialism, nationalism and a growing disenchantment with religious formalism and the Church's antiquated attitudes. As for attitudes in Perth, it is ironic to note that while the Rev C Robertson of St Andrew's Parish Church died from wounds sustained at Salonica, the RC clergy of Perth refused to join their Episcopal brethren of St Ninian's Cathedral in weekly intercessory prayers for peace. Some might have found it hard to believe in religion after that. What did survive from the war was a strange blend of mysticism, fundamental evangelism, nihilism and pacifism - a totally useless brew for the problems of the 1930s.

Difficult to deal with is the question of whether the First World War gave women greater social freedom. The question is simplistic, because, in Perth at least, there were class variations. Upper-class women in Perth clearly regarded the war as an extension of their charity work to help the less fortunate, hence their heavy involvement in a mass of committees and clubs. Middle-class women, especially those married to professional men, had, for a change, to collect their own shopping, do their own washing and cook their own meals. No doubt this goes some way to explaining the more humane treatment of servants after the war. Young middle-class women, on the other hand, saw the war as an opportunity to escape family restraints and the stifling conventions of their hometowns. For a while it was great fun to drive a tram or an ambulance, and, after all, it was helping the war effort and was not considered a disgrace.

Working-class women in Perth were hardly touched by the war. They still had long, backbreaking hours in Pullars or Shields and then it was back home to feed the children, wash their clothes and clean the house. The fact that the health of so many improved during the war was not due to a better diet but to the end of the old tradition of giving the most and the best to the male wage-earner. As he was in France, both wives and children were the better for it. Sadly, it did not last and with demobilisation, the old ways returned.

Drink and rough language, however unusual and disturbing to middle-class girls, was the rule for the factory floor and the pub-crawl existed in Perth long before 1914 as far as women were concerned. Little refinements came more from the cinema, and other results of 19th century industrialisation, rather than the war. It was the films that taught self-awareness and poise, a new form of speech (Americanism) and the use of cosmetics. A modern form of escapism, the cinema, was even better than drink. Magazines had a similar impact. As for careers, lower middle-class girls owed far more to the typewriter and shorthand than the war for their position in an office in the city. It was the same with sexual freedom stimulated by the bicycle, a 19th century product. This, far more than the First World War, killed off the old tradition of chaperones. Indeed, the bicycle even influenced dress. A long skirt made cycling difficult and a corset made it impossible, hence the bra. Again, if munitions' work is supposed to have liberated many women, it certainly brought a lot more eczema and anaemia. It is often forgotten by commentators, that Perth, like Dundee, had long been a factory town employing mainly women who were married with families.

But, what about the vote? Did women win the franchise because of the war? In Perth at least, the war delayed the suffrage for women. This had not been at any time a matter of justice: it was simply politics. The Liberal Government was plainly afraid of how women would use their vote. The Tories opposed it as well because of their opposition to Irish Home Rule. Ulster merely confirmed the Government's suspicions. Yet, in Perth, every leading figure, both Liberal and Unionist, was in favour of extending the franchise. The Perth newspapers all pointed out time and time again that Australia had granted an extension of the franchise in 1902, Finland in 1906 and Norway in 1913. Denmark and Iceland, neutral countries, granted the suffrage in 1915. Clearly then, the gift of franchise depended on local circumstances. It is even probable that a faster growth of the Labour Party would have granted it sooner. Did militancy then damage the women's cause? Probably not. Born of frustration and impatience, their cause failed through lack of unity, and even more so, lack of clear policy. Sadly, when women were granted the franchise following a long and gallant struggle, they made little of it. Few wanted to enter politics although they had campaigned noisily for the freedom to do so in Perth since 1872.

It is customary to make much of the increased powers of the State during the First World War. As far as Perth was concerned, however, the State had interfered extensively in people's affairs by 1908 with its provisions for children and again in 1909 with the Cinematograph Film Act. The latter was the reason for the construction of specialised picture-houses and the closure of sub-standard premises. The best example of the State's ever-increasing muscle was the setting up of the British Board of Film Censors in 1913. This offered a hint of future developments. A strange but oft-repeated claim is that the war stimulated the growth of the Labour Party. In Perth, it was the direct opposite. In 1899 the Conservatives' main campaigning platform was 'Protection'. Few believed in it. By 1919, following the experience of war, with the desire to avoid foreign entanglements, a wish to strengthen imperial bonds and a deep-rooted belief in the racial superiority of the Anglo-Saxons, the Conservative numbers in Perth steadily grew. The Liberals, who had long dominated every aspect of life in the city found themselves heading for the wilderness because of internal divisions, their adherence to a discredited belief in Free Trade, and, worst of all, the rise of a working-class group, the Labour Party.

The latter had a substantial pre-1914 track record in Perth. Founded in 1907 they were vociferous in their condemnation of slums and high rents, but they failed in their bid to win over the Perth trade unions. And, in that, they never did succeed. This was partly due to their flirtation with the USSR in the romantic post-war period and their ignoring the fact that the people of Perth openly loathed the Soviet system. Only the trade unions could give them the strength to overcome these attitudes and Perth was not sufficiently industrialised for that. Besides, by 1922, it was obvious that political polarisation would make the acceptance of the Labour Party as a popular choice harder to achieve.

There is no doubt that the standard of living in Perth rose during the war because wages were doubled, particularly during the later stages of the conflict. Naturally, the highest rises went to the poorest paid. Those outside the war economy did not share in this bonanza, particularly the building and textile workers. Differentials fell rapidly as bonuses were paid as a flat rate. Briefly, the picture was this: rampant inflation between 1913 and 1920, that is, inflation which started before the war; a rapid fall between 1920 and 1922; and then a moderate fall between 1922 and 1932. Contemporaries were mystified by this pattern although they should not have been. Prices behaved exactly the same way after the Boer War. Analysis shows that food prices began to sneak upwards in Perth as early as 1906 and then, suddenly, leaping with a bound in 1911. The coal strike of 1912 actually led to the wage-scramble of 1913. After the war and the end of price controls, the position worsened. It was not until just before 1914 that Perth Town Council decided to tackle seriously the problem of poverty. Over the war years, the deferential attitude towards the poor began to dissolve. Fewer now lived on the subsistence border and more money went on food than ever before. There was a high level of rent control and families were smaller. There was little unemployment, and, best of all, there were separation allowances for soldiers' wives. Thus, the Prince of Wales' Relief Fund was not actually needed in Perth as poverty had dwindled. Unfortunately, by 1921, poverty was on the return and its cause was unemployment.

The standard view of trade unions is that they made their great advances in the post-war period with violence and militancy. As far as Perth is concerned, they had been gathering strength since 1906 trying to create a social revolution by stages. In 1909 the trade unions argued that Lloyd George should have gone further in his revolutionary budget and in 1911 they demanded rises when the cost of living rose. But it was in 1910 that they started their big push to win Perth. They knew that the Dyers' Union, potentially the largest, was the key and they used their best organisers, Hayhurst, Dallas, Brown, Macarthur, Rushworth, McLean and Sloan, to win it. The turning point came with the rail strike of 1911 when Perth was paralysed. This showed the way. Unity was strength. By 1913, they were in the process of launching their second attack on the matter of closed shops when the war came. In 1919, they simply continued their pre-war militancy which the violence at Stanley and Huntingtower should not obscure. By the 1920s, their numbers were high in Perth. Then, with the cutbacks of 1921 and the trade unions' inability to do anything, their numbers fell away again in Perth.

Industry in Perth was marked in the immediate pre-war years by a move to limited liability company formats. This marked the end of the old family style of management dear to the hearts of the Pullars, Campbells and Shields. Pullars in particular suffered from an inherent defect: geographical isolation. This made the North British Dye Works and her local competitors helpless in the face of rail and coal strikes. In fact, these together did more damage to the economy of Perth than the enemy with the dye blockade. Only a reduction in their labour-intensive work and a switch to laundry might have saved them. It is therefore false to blame the war and the stirring events of the Battle of the Gates in 1917 for a decline which had begun long before, probably around 1904.

If proof were needed that conditions were changing it could be found in the post-war prosperity of the General Accident Insurance Company which saw a sharp rise in share-profits, entirely due to rapid expansion of motor insurance. By 1922 the dyeing industry is clearly in decline, and this despite every technique of modern management including the 8 a.m start, works' councils, staff conferences, massive advertising, pension, sickness and holiday schemes. In a desperate attempt to save the situation, cutbacks and probationary regulations pushed industrial relations back to the days before 1914.

Much in post-war Perth had not changed. As far as the people were concerned, an alien was an alien and not to be trusted, especially a German. Now, even the French fell into that category. Crime had quickly recovered its place in police statistics, despite what sociologists might think about the loss of innocence and the growth of cynicism. Judging by police files, there was vandalism in Perth in 1851 and train hooliganism in 1863. There were no signs of much change in morality, but just a few in terms of the law. Prostitutes still lurked on the Inches and the family was subjected to as much strain as before the war. Young men still enlisted in the Army and everything seemed much as it was before.

Surely, one has to ask, there must be some lessons to emerge from this study of war? Indeed, there are. In brief, they are as follows. Change, as the truism says, is not progress and one must always remember that, particularly as faulty memory makes us selective in our recall and thus continually form myths. Incredibly, modern scholars, historians and sociologists, who pride themselves on their devotion to the task of exposing such follies, create others in their turn.

Commonsense should have told us all that wars affect different regions in different ways and that it is a thankless and impossible task to distinguish long-term trends from the continuum of war. It appears that the effects of any war can be exaggerated. That this is so is proved by the speedy recovery of the combatants. Even the fields of Flanders bear no sign today of violent conflict. Despite the equally obvious fact that 'total war' has nothing to do with industrialisation, but everything to do with lack of restraint, then 'total war' is not new. It is as old as time itself. As for our modern society, the motorcar and the film had greater effect by far on our cities, our manners and our lives than the war. Technology shapes our destiny, not wars. Indeed, wars act rather as a brake on development than as an accelerator. Perhaps the most lasting effects of war are psychological, a mixture of grief, guilt and memory. It is this mixture, as Ortega y Gasset said, 'which enters the soul of man.'

Books from Cualann Press

Under the Shadow
Letters of Love and War 1911-1917
The Poignant Testimony and Story
of
Hugh Wallace Mann
7th & 5th Battalions
The Queen's Own Cameron Highlanders
and
Jessie Reid

Narrative: Bríd Hetherington

'A sensitively-handled presentation, with introductions to each chapter giving the background to events.' The Scots Magazine

ISBN 0 9535036 0 7
£12.99